William Frederick Poole
and the Modern Library Movement

Number Thirteen
Columbia University Studies
in Library Service

William Frederick Poole
and the
Modern Library Movement

by William Landram Williamson

Columbia University Press
New York and London 1963

William Landram Williamson is Butler Librarian at Columbia University. He received his M.S. degree from the Columbia University School of Library Service in 1949 and his Ph.D. from the University of Chicago Graduate Library School in 1959. His doctoral dissertation formed the basis for the present work.

Columbia University Studies in Library Service

Preface

On an obscure stair-landing in the Chicago Public Library stands a bust of William Frederick Poole. A patron might visit the library regularly for many years without ever seeing that memorial to its first librarian. Few serious library users could fail, however, to become aware of *Poole's Index* or, at the least, the *Readers' Guide to Periodical Literature* of which it was the pioneering forerunner. In the same way, Poole the pioneer librarian is little known. And yet his mark is still upon the Boston Athenaeum, the Cincinnati Public Library, the Chicago Public Library, and the Newberry Library, all of which he headed. In a less clear way, his mark is still on many other libraries whose development he encouraged. Even in faraway Norway, libraries are still using methods introduced by Poole in the Chicago Public Library and carried back by Haakon Nyhuus, who learned them during service in Chicago.

Poole was a man of stature both in the library world and in the world of scholarship. He was president of both the American Library Association and the American Historical Association. He was the author of many periodical articles and book reviews and of a number of books. His theories concerning Cotton Mather's part in Salem witchcraft and Manasseh Cutler's part in the Ordinance of 1787 are among his writings which still receive the respectful attention of scholars. His days were spent in libraries and his nights in indexing and writing.

Poole was a man of learning, but he was no pale bookish scholar. He was a man of force and courage, warmth and humor. The reader will look in vain, however, for a well-rounded and complete picture of Poole the man in this book. He was too proud and self-contained to give more than hints of his personal feelings in public or business communications. And almost none of his private communications survives. But evidence of Poole the man exists in the testimony of those who knew him as well as in the flashes of humor that shine out in his recorded speeches and writings.

Although occasional glimpses of the human being will be found in this book, it is primarily a case study of the librarian whose career epitomized library development in the United States during the last half of the nineteenth century. It is based upon the much longer doctoral dissertation written under the direction of Howard W. Winger and submitted in 1959 to the Graduate Library School of the University of Chicago. The reader who wishes exhaustive detail and complete documentation is referred to that study. Notes in the present book are limited primarily to sources of quotations.

The officials of many libraries have made available their resources and helped in the use of their collections. For this assistance and for permission to consult, quote, or refer to manuscript materials, grateful acknowledgment is made to the following: *

Connecticut
  Yale University Library, New Haven
    Yale Memorabilia Room
District of Columbia
  Library of Congress, Washington
    American Historical Association Papers
    Benjamin Holt Ticknor Papers
  Smithsonian Institution, Washington
Illinois
  Charles Evans Papers under the control of Eliot H. Evans, Chicago
  Chicago Historical Society
  Chicago Public Library
    Administrative Files
  Evanston Public Library
  Newberry Library, Chicago
    Poole Papers
  Northwestern University Library, Evanston
  University of Chicago Library
  University of Illinois Library, Urbana
Indiana
  Indianapolis Public Library

Maryland
  Johns Hopkins University Library, Baltimore
    Daniel Coit Gilman Papers

* Specific collections of papers listed are only the principal sources of value in the institutions named. Other Poole letters are frequently to be found elsewhere in these libraries.

Herbert B. Adams Papers
Maryland Historical Society, Baltimore
Peabody Institute of Baltimore
United States Naval Academy Library, Annapolis
Massachusetts
American Antiquarian Society, Worcester
Clarence W. Bowen Papers
George Watson Cole Papers
Librarians' Incoming Correspondence
Boston Athenaeum
Boston Public Library
Manuscript material used by courtesy of the Trustees of the Boston Public Library
Boston University Library
Mercantile Library Association records
Essex Institute, Salem
Harvard University Library, Cambridge
Harvard Archives
Houghton Library
Massachusetts Historical Society, Boston
Charles Deane Papers
Winsor's *Memorial History of Boston* scrapbooks
Winsor's *Narrative and Critical History* scrapbooks
Melrose Public Library
Worcester Public Library
Minnesota
Minnesota Historical Society, Minneapolis
New York
Columbia University Libraries, New York
Melvil Dewey Papers
Grosvenor Library, Buffalo
Administrative Files
New York Public Library
Ford Papers
Lenox Library Papers
Ohio
Cincinnati Literary Club
Dayton Public Library
Historical and Philosophical Society of Ohio, Cincinnati
Gallipolis Papers
Public Library of Cincinnati
Rutherford B. Hayes Library, Fremont
Pennsylvania
Historical Society of Pennsylvania, Philadelphia
Public Library of Philadelphia

Rhode Island
  Brown University Library, Providence
Wisconsin
  State Historical Society of Wisconsin, Madison
    Lyman C. Draper Papers
    McCormick Historical Association
Canada
  Public Archives of Canada, Ottawa
    Douglas Brymner Papers
England
  British Museum

A list of all of the individuals in these institutions and else-where who have given generous assistance would be long indeed. The earnest desire and impressive capacity to help patrons is one of the happy characteristics of American librarians. The gratitude to all of these people is very real. I also wish to acknowledge here the assistance and encouragement of the many others who helped me in this work.

Publication of this book is made possible, in part, by a grant from the Newberry Library which, in this way, honors its founding librarian.

W. L. W.

March, 1963

Contents

Illustrations

William Frederick Poole
and the Modern Library Movement

I. The Years of Preparation

William Frederick Poole was born in Salem, Massachusetts, on December 24, 1821, the second son of Ward and Eliza Wilder Poole. Although the Pooles had lived in the community for generations, they were not a part of the romantic and prosperous Salem of sailing ships and the East India trade; they lived and worked among the tanners in Poole's—sometimes called Blubber—Hollow near the outskirts of the city. The section was soon transferred to the adjoining town of Danvers, so that it was in the common schools of that community that young Will received his early education. He learned the basic skills of literacy and, together with some other promising students, was given special instruction in such additional subjects as astronomy, geometry, algebra, and Latin.

Although Will was a bright pupil, he left school at the age of twelve just as most of his fellows did. In 1834 he was sent to his mother's home town of Keene, New Hampshire, where his grandfather Abel Wilder still lived and where the youngster was apprenticed to a cousin, Edward Poole, who kept a jewelry store on the town square. At the end of a year, Will rejoined his family for a move to a farm near Worcester in central Massachusetts. After a year on the farm, he returned to Danvers to work, first, in a grain and provision store and, later, as a teamster for a tannery.

When Will was seventeen, he decided, at his mother's urging, to return to school and entered Leicester Academy near Worcester in the autumn of 1839. After three years of study there and some teaching experience, he went to New Haven in 1842 to enter Yale College.

As a young man of twenty, Will Poole was older than many of his fellow students, in a day when college entrance at fourteen was not uncommon. His basic education in the Danvers school had given him a solid scholastic grounding. When he went to Leicester Academy, his maturity had enabled him to take full advantage of his college preparatory studies. His experience as a teacher had given him a special perspective on the educative process and also that firm grasp of subject matter which only teaching can provide. His scholastic accomplishments had given him a foundation on which to build further knowledge of subject disciplines and their bibliographies. His tannery work had acquainted him with the merits and defects of various kinds of leathers which, during most of his library career, he would find were used as the standard book-binding material. His mercantile experience had furnished him with a knowledge of business methods. Most important, his varied background had given him an ability to deal with practical men of affairs and had helped to instill in him the common sense and the pragmatic approach to problems which were to characterize his whole career. Though he went to college later than many of his fellows, his years of moving about from job to job had been useful to him.

Yale College in 1842 was, like other colleges of the time, a place of tradition and conservatism. Its buildings, its faculty, and its curriculum linked the present with the distant past. The purpose of education was to strengthen and discipline the mind; factual knowledge was secondary. The subjects of the classical curriculum were primarily Latin, Greek, and mathematics, although philosophy, history, political economy, and a few other subjects held a minor place. Class time was devoted to recitation and lesson-hearing. It was dull rote-work, but it was, to a degree, effective. Students did learn Latin, Greek, and mathematics; their minds were awakened, improved, and disciplined. Not the best student in his class, Poole stood nevertheless in its upper half at the end of his first year at Yale.

Despite his good showing, the young man was prevented by financial difficulties from continuing his studies. It was only after three years of working and saving that he could return to college in May, 1846, shortly before the class with which he had entered was to graduate. Poole joined the Class of 1849 in the last term of its freshman year, presumably as a way of reviewing before the start of the sophomore year. His additional maturity seems to have helped him in his studies. Whereas he had been only in the upper half of his freshman class, he was twentieth of ninety-six students during the review term and fourteenth of more than a hundred during the sophomore year. Late in that year, Poole entered the work which, if it later reduced his scholastic standing somewhat, laid the foundations for his reputation and career. He was appointed assistant librarian of the student society called the Brothers in Unity.

The Brothers Library was one of several libraries on the Yale campus at the time. From the point of view of the students, it was considerably more useful than the college's own library. Fundamentally, this was true by deliberate intent. The college president told Poole and his classmates in a fatherly lecture that "a student who designed to make study subordinate to reading might better stay at home and buy the books he wished to read with the money it cost to stay in College." [1] In this statement, the president reflected the virtually universal conviction that wide reading, as contrasted with close study of the prescribed textbooks, should be actively discouraged. Poole recalled: "Books, outside of the textbooks used, had no part in our education. They were never quoted, recommended, nor mentioned by the instructors in the classroom." [2] The upperclassmen could use the college library only after the payment of a special fee, and the freshmen and sophomores were not allowed to use it at all. The Brothers Library was considerably closer to the life of the students, as was the Society of which it was a part.

The Society of the Brothers in Unity was one of three competing organizations. These societies occupied a central place in the life of the college. Since there were no organized athletics and since student government, even to the extent of electing class officers, was specifically forbidden, there were few organized channels for noncurricular activities. One of the few doors to distinction outside the classroom lay in the forensic exercises sponsored by the societies or by the college. An educated man had a responsibility not only to know more than other citizens but to be able to express himself and to hold his own in rough-and-tumble argument. Florid oratory was in fashion, and a college graduate had to be prepared to take his place among the leaders in the pulpits and legislative halls. Of the three societies which fostered this ability, the smallest was the Calliopean, which students from the South joined as a matter of course. For the membership of the rest of the student body, the Linonian Society and the Society of Brothers in Unity competed vigorously. Regardless of which society a student joined, he found the activities essentially the same. In meetings held every Wednesday evening, the societies served as the platforms for passionate debate. Was slavery wrong? Would the nation ever become truly free? Had Napoleon's exile to St. Helena been just? What should be done about the new Texas Republic? Subjects like these were hotly argued in debates between members of the same society or in competition between the societies.

To provide ammunition for debates, the societies had collected libraries. As years passed, the students—and the faculty as well— turned here also for their recreational reading. These collections were, in the college community, parallels to the social libraries of the cities and towns of New England. Just as local communities felt no obligation to provide books for their citizens, so the college felt no responsibility to supply its students. And, just as citizens of other communities banded together to provide for their own needs, so the students of Yale in their societies assembled libraries. Even the origin of the need for books in debating is reminiscent of the beginnings of the Philadelphia Library Company in Benjamin Franklin's Junto or of the Redwood Library in the Philosophical Society of Newport, Rhode Island. And, as the municipalities often took over the social libraries as a part of the public libraries, Yale eventually gathered the society collections into the college library. But this merger did not take place until a number of years later. In 1847, the societies were still independent, vigorous institutions.

The independence of the society libraries had been at issue the previous year when the college authorities had invited the societies to move their libraries into its imposing new library building. After receiving formal assurance that the move implied no loss of sovereignty, the societies had accepted and so had acquired handsome new quarters. The building was composed of three parallel structures resembling Gothic chapels and connected by hall-like wings across the front. The central structure was the largest and housed the college library; the two dominant societies occupied the smaller structures to the right and left. The Calliopean

Society was assigned one of the wings, with the college librarian using the other wing as his office and reception room.

As a result of these moves, the Brothers Library in which Poole began his work was housed in a long, rectangular room. Near the entrance, a railing set off a delivery area beyond which patrons were not allowed to go. The books were kept on shelves in twenty alcoves, ten on the main floor and ten in galleries. During the half hour between one-thirty and two o'clock each afternoon when the library was open, the librarians fetched the books requested and checked them out to the students. Although the patrons were forbidden to go to the shelves, the regulations in the Brothers Library were considerably more liberal than those in the college library, where use of books in the building was encouraged in preference to lending and where underclassmen were not allowed at all. In their own society libraries, all classes of students could borrow as many as four books, including bound periodicals, for two weeks, with the privilege of one renewal.

Poole was fortunate in having his first experience in such a library. He said that they were the "most profitable years" [8] that he had spent in libraries, but this was not in a financial sense. While by no means all problems of library management had been worked out, it was a functioning organization which he could observe and in which he could make experiments in methods. Moreover, it was, for its day, unusually devoted to service to its patrons.

The principal service for which the library was created was to provide help in finding material for debates. As each debate topic was announced in chapel, the librarians were called upon by the students for assistance. Since the requests were recurrent, the librarians began to keep a record of the materials they had found useful on certain questions and to post in the library lists of references on the current question. In January of 1847, a compilation of such lists had been published in an eight-page pamphlet bearing the title *Subjects for Debate, with References to Authorities.* The booklet was prepared by John Edmands, then the Brothers librarian and, later, librarian of the Philadelphia Mercantile Library. It contained citations to books and magazine articles under topics such as "Is a Lie Ever Justifiable?" or "Is England Rising or Falling as a Nation?"

The publication was the first of a remarkable group of bibliographical aids prepared by the student-librarians of the Brothers Library, each an adumbration of a later basic library tool. Edmands's work might loosely be considered a forerunner of the Debaters' Handbook series of the H. W. Wilson Company. Poole himself prepared a periodical index that foreshadowed its own later editions and the series of Wilson indexes. A third publication was an index to essays and parts of books, a pioneer *Essay and General Literature Index,* prepared by Albert Hebard in connection with his work on the library's 1851 catalog to which it was an appendix. Before the catalog could be published, Hebard died, as the result—so his contemporaries thought—of exhaustion brought on by the work. Each publication was a pioneering venture spurred on by what were evidently powerful forces. Though each was the work of an individual impelled by the imponderables of his own personality, there were other, more evident factors behind them.

These factors may be found in the dominant character of the time and in the local scene at Yale College. What Poole called the "motive that inspired me" [4] was "a youthful impulse to do something that ought to be done." [5] The religious and moral spirit of the age put upon every man the duty to serve God by making the world a better place and upon an educated man a special responsibility to the world of scholarship. There was, moreover, the natural desire of individuals to excel. The student-librarians were paid to perform their regular duties, but these additional tasks were undertaken in a spirit of service, tempered in its altruism by a wish for recognition. In carrying out their projects, the young librarians were guided by a pragmatism which caused them to seek solutions to their problems untrammeled by any bondage to blazed trails. And, indeed, what paths existed were marked out only faintly. To these forces was added the impetus to improvement given by the new library building. The prospect of clean, spacious, new quarters naturally made the custodians turn to efforts to make the libraries match their surroundings. It is significant that all three of the societies published new catalogs of their collections in 1846, about the time they moved into the new building. All of these motives, and perhaps others too, led the young librarians to do something beyond their day-to-day duties. But there were also conditions in the normal routine that made bibliographical work an important need.

Since the library was operated on the closed-shelf principle with no subject arrangement of books on the shelves, some indexing medium was needed. The patrons requested the books they wanted by means of the arbitrary number assigned to each volume in the library. They had to know in advance precisely what books they wanted, for they had no opportunity to browse among the books on the shelves. The 1846 catalog of the library provided an up-to-date key to the volumes in the collection by author and by title, and, in addition, its index gave a broad subject approach to the monographs. For the contents of periodicals, there was not even a rudimentary key. The students were left dependent upon their own memories, the recommendations of the librarians, indexes to single volumes, and a few general indexes to individual magazines.

This deficiency was a source of trouble to the librarians and to the patrons. The students made "many and annoying inquiries for 'something on the Hartford Convention,' 'Capital Punishment,' 'the Tariff,' 'Thomas Jefferson,' etc. etc." Even with the help of the librarians, the students "spent hours in *guessing* what books contained the desired information, without finding the right ones, and [were] tempted to believe that College Libraries had nothing but their number of volumes to recommend them." [6] At times, the librarians were able to help, but often volumes were brought from the shelves at the request of a student who found upon examining them that they contained nothing useful to him. The librarians then had to return these volumes to the shelves and get others. Since the library was open for only half an hour each day, there was little time for a student to examine many volumes before making up his mind which ones he would take. Even more serious than the inconvenience, the students frequently went away annoyed and disappointed, thinking the library had nothing useful to them, when, in fact, it did. "The sets of standard periodicals with which the library was well supplied were not used, although they were rich in the treatment of subjects about which inquiries were made in vain every day." [7] Thus, the need for some adequate way to help the students was apparent.

Edmands's little booklet was a step in the direction of better bibliographical control, but it was useful only for those topics for which he had prepared lists of references. The trouble with Edmands's work was that, every time a new topic was debated, a new search had to be made through the books and the periodical volumes. It was a subject bibliography, not an index. If a true index to the contents of periodicals were made, it would be necessary only to look under the appropriate subjects when a new debate topic was announced. Poole determined to prepare such an index.

Poole's project was especially appropriate at the time, because magazines had taken their place as an important form of publication during the immediately preceding years. Although the first American magazine had been published a century before and perhaps a hundred different ones had been started before 1800, their circulation was limited, and the life of any one of them was brief. Not until 1811 did any American magazine survive to celebrate its tenth anniversary. In the first quarter of the nineteenth century, perhaps as many as 600 were started, but, again, most were short-lived. In 1825, something under 100 were being published. By contrast, the twenty-five years up to 1850 saw 4,000 to 5,000 started, and, at mid-century, about 600 were in existence. A few journals had achieved enough stability to survive for long periods. Magazines like *North American Review, American Journal of Science,* and *Christian Examiner,* established before 1825, were still vigorous in 1850. *Graham's Magazine, Knickerbocker Magazine, Southern Literary Messenger,* and others established after 1825, were still active. Most important, these journals contained significant literary, scientific, and political discussions by the leading writers of the time. Poole did not overstate the case when he said that

periodical publications have been gradually advancing in merit, until, for ability and influence, they have come in our day to stand in the front rank of modern literature. There is scarcely any subject in philosophy or criticism, the sciences or the arts, politics or religion, that has not been discussed in them by the first writers of the age. . . . In the investigation of a subject, an able article in a review is often more useful to the student than a professed treatise.[8]

Nor was this importance limited to American periodicals. Various English journals, like *Edinburgh Review, Blackwood's Magazine,* and *Westminster Review,* were so popular, and the protection offered by the copyright laws so slight, that the volumes were regularly pirated in the United States, both by reprints of the complete periodicals and by reproductions of selections from foreign magazines in a number of eclectic journals.

Poole set himself the task of providing a way for the users of the Brothers Library to find this valuable material. His first production was a modest manuscript index to perhaps two hundred periodical volumes. Though it was, as Poole admitted, "crude and feeble on its bibliographical side," the manuscript was a new and unique instrument providing access to a group of writings which had been, for most practical purposes, useless. It brought to the library "the whole body of students for a kind of help they could not get from the library catalogues, nor from any other source." [9] But there were disadvantages. Since there was only one copy, only one person could consult it at a time, yet it was in such constant use that the manuscript began to wear out. If it were printed, the fruits of Poole's work would be preserved and made available more widely and more conveniently.

Once the decision to print had been made, the young librarian set out to expand and correct his manuscript. He reexamined all the volumes covered previously and indexed many new periodicals, tripling the size of his original manuscript. His method was to work systematically through each volume in turn, indexing as he went. Ignoring the magazines' own indexes, he worked directly with the articles, actually reading through them when necessary to determine the subject being considered. For those articles that he selected as being useful to the patrons of the library, he made an entry consisting of a shortened, catchword title, the volume number and name of the periodical, the initial page of the article, and the call number of the volume in the Brothers Library. All entries were under the catchword subject; there were no entries by author. But the name of the writer was included in the entry for some articles, primarily those by prominent authors or by men connected with Yale. This information was not always easy to obtain, since the articles in the review magazines were usually unsigned. Anonymity of authorship was beginning to be abandoned in the general magazines, but it was still maintained in the review journals, even though the authorship of articles in the current issues was often a matter of common knowledge.

The use of entry wording that adhered closely to the language of the titles of the articles was a distinctive characteristic of the Poole indexes; he made no attempt to prepare a standard list of subject headings so as to gather together all material on a given topic under a single subject entry, though he did include some cross references. Whatever defects this procedure may have had in scattering citations to articles on the same subject in accordance with the verbal whims of the authors, it had the positive virtue of permitting the indexing to be done quickly. Poole was not faced with the constant need to make decisions about the proper subject heading to use, since he generally used a word from the actual title. There were, of course, some articles with vague titles for which he had to provide an entry. Working as he did without any list of subject headings, he found that he must keep in mind what entries he had used previously in order to select the most useful catchword when there was a choice. He could best remember what he had done if he worked regularly without periods of inactivity. When he did so, the task became a kind of play. Since he completed each volume as he went along, he could have the satisfaction of seeing a growing pile of indexed volumes.

Even though the task had its satisfactions, it was demanding. Between July of 1847 when Poole became assistant librarian and July of 1848 when the first printed edition was published, he prepared the manuscript index, revised and expanded it for printing, made a fair copy of the whole for the printer, and, as a final step, checked each entry in the proof sheets with the original volumes to ensure accuracy. In order to keep up with this heavy load, he had to work until the early morning hours, frequently getting a few hours of rest before the beginning of the next day by sleeping fully clothed on one of the library tables. The burden was great because the indexing was done in addition to his regular responsibilities in the library and in the classroom.

Poole's classroom work showed the effects of the time spent on his indexing. His grade average declined during the three quarters of the junior year, reaching the low point of his college career during the final quarter, when he was busily making preparations for publication of the *Index*. Nevertheless, his over-all grades during his first three years placed him twenty-second out of ninety-four students in his class, winning him election to Phi Beta Kappa and selection to deliver an oration at the Junior Exhibition. Appropriately for one who became noted for his pragmatism, the topic of the oration was "Utility."

Besides these honors earned on the basis of faculty judgments, Poole was chosen by his fellows as one of thirteen juniors elected to Alpha Delta Phi, one of the secret societies. Among his classmates also chosen were Timothy Dwight, who became president of Yale, and Franklin W. Fisk, who became president of the Chicago Theological Seminary. If Poole's selection to this honor was a reflection of the esteem of his fellows, one faculty member's action showed the interest in him taken by his tutors. Professor James Luce Kingsley, the venerable Latin teacher, came into the library one day and handed Poole a slip of paper bearing a motto which he had composed in honor of the *Index*. The phrase, *Qui scit ubi sit scientia, habenti est proximus* (He who knows where knowledge dwells has it within his reach), eventually appeared on the title page of every edition.

Before a book bearing the new motto could be published, the problem of finance had to be solved. Poole tried to attract subscriptions to pay the costs by issuing a circular describing the plan, but the effort was not successful. At this juncture, Henry Stevens, a former Brothers librarian who was on his way to becoming a famed bookdealer, interceded for Poole with George Palmer Putnam, who was launching a publishing house in New York. Putnam agreed to supply the necessary funds, and, when the book appeared early in July, it bore the imprint of his company.

The new book was a small volume indexing selectively articles appearing in 560 volumes of thirty-one different publications. It was neither complete nor comprehensive, but, being made for a particular audience by one closely in touch with its needs and interests, it served a useful purpose. Its importance, however, lies in its position as a historic milestone. It was a new and unique instrument of bibliographical control, the general index to a number of different periodicals in one alphabet. It inaugurated a bibliographical form which became one of the basic cornerstones of library service in the United States.

The book's value was so readily recognized that the whole edition of five hundred copies was soon sold. Encouraged by the response, Poole determined to prepare an enlarged edition. He continued to work in the library, having been elected librarian for the ensuing year. It was a tribute to his practical judgment that the members took the unusual step of reelecting him, as he had been elected the previous year, to serve as one of the three members of the society's Prudential Committee. This group was in charge of the practical and monetary affairs of the society, including the library, so that Poole during these years was in a sense both employer and employee. His work with the library and with the indexing was little hampered by the class work of the senior year. Attaining to membership in the senior class was itself deemed a distinction. The classes were taught only by the professors, who made less exacting demands than had the earnest young tutors. Poole had time and freedom to devote to his other interests. He did not complete the indexing, however, so that at the end of the year, when he relinquished his duties as librarian and would no longer have access to the library as a student, he was formally granted the privilege of continuing to use it to finish his work.

As a graduating senior, Poole was confronted by the same problem which faced his classmates. He was presumed to be ready to go out into the world to make a living. Ten years had passed since his mother had persuaded him that he should prepare himself for college. Now he had finished his college work, but he had no clear goal. Not that he feared the future. He observed to one of his classmates:

We are now *men*, and must be known, if we are known at all, *as men*. For my own part, I do not regret that we have finished our college studies; not that I expect pleasanter days than I have spent in Old Yale or that I shall find warmer or truer friends, but I long to be engaged in the great strife of life. My philosophy is not to mope and whine over the *past* but to look for happiness in the future. I have ever observed that my capacity for enjoyment increased with my knowledge and my years and I have no fear that now the rule will be reversed.[10]

Though he did not fear the future, it was still uncertain. Most young men graduating from college in those days entered one of the three learned professions; more than two thirds of the graduates became lawyers, physicians, or ministers. Poole was not sure what he was going to do. If he had thoughts of becoming a librarian, no record of the fact remains. He told his friend that he would "probably be settled in the Law somewhere in Massachusetts." [11]

Poole's prediction for his future was realized only in part; he did settle in Massachusetts, but not as a lawyer. It is difficult to account for the slow tempo of the next two years of his life in the light of the vigor and speed with which he worked at other times in his career. He seems to have decided to complete the new edition of the *Index* rather than take a regular job. His notes were made in an interleaved copy of the first edition. One evening in Worcester, during 1850, he carelessly left the volume in the buggy while he went into the City Hall to hear a speech by Charles Allen, the local Congressman. When he returned, the book was gone. Even this staggering loss did not stop him. In 1851 he had the work well on the way to completion when a new opportunity opened up for him. The assistant librarian of the Boston Athenaeum was forced by ill health to take a leave of absence. Poole was employed as his temporary successor.

The Athenaeum, though a private library, was one of the largest and best in the country. There Poole worked under Charles Folsom, a former librarian of Harvard College and the Athenaeum's librarian since 1846. Folsom kept himself aloof from daily operations so that Poole himself was "the business man in the Library" and performed the regular duties of serving the patrons and keeping the accounts. He continued to work on the *Index* and put his manuscript to good use in helping the patrons of the Athenaeum find magazine articles. His service at the Athenaeum lasted only a few months, but it had the effect of pleasing his employers with his work and settling his mind as to a career. He proposed to "pursue bibliography as a profession." [12]

In line with that decision, he considered seeking appointment as librarian of the proposed public library of Boston and at the Astor Library in New York. The position he obtained was, however, at the Mercantile Library Association of Boston where, on May 31, 1852, he was elected librarian.

II. The Start of a Career, 1852-1856

During the next four years, Poole began to settle into a routine of life. He had his regular duties as librarian of the Mercantile Library Association. He finished and published the second edition of his *Index*. He prepared and published a pioneering catalog of his library. He married and began to raise a family. After having lived in various places, he moved to a house on Emerson Street in Melrose, which he made his home during the rest of his stay in Boston. The position at the Mercantile Library gave him the opportunity to become established in his personal and professional life.

The Mercantile Library Association of Boston was the oldest of its type in the country, having been founded on March 11, 1820. Its members were young employees of the business houses of the city. A subscription library, with membership open to any young man working in business and willing to pay the annual $2.00 fee, it was a democratic organization. Membership fees were only one of its sources of income; annual lecture series produced a balance considerably above the cost of hall rentals and speakers' fees. In addition, the merchants and philanthropists of the city considered it their paternalistic duty to help to support the association. In 1852, when Poole became librarian, the association had a large and active membership and a considerable treasury.

In its purposes, the Mercantile Library Association of Boston was like some fifteen similar groups in the country at the time. It sought to train young men for advancement in business careers, it provided wholesome recreation, and it tried to give its young members a cultural background appropriate to their hoped-for positions in the world. By arrangement with a local school, members were eligible for special reduced tuition for business and language courses relevant to work in commerce in a seaboard community. The annual lecture series presented such distinguished speakers as Edward Everett, Oliver Wendell Holmes, and Henry Ward Beecher, along with others of less enduring fame. The members themselves participated in weekly literary meetings.

In addition to giving courses and lectures, the association fostered the cultural growth of its members by maintaining a library, which one of its presidents characterized as "the most important feature . . . the central idea around which the others all cluster—the main trunk from which the others spring." Lectures, newspaper reading rooms, and other features of the association might be, at times, more popular, but nothing could take the place of the library, where members could obtain a "complete and comprehensive knowledge of the subject treated" and a "lasting impression upon the mind." The association must depend upon the library "for its permanency, and for its greatest, if not its most apparent usefulness." [1]

In selecting a chief officer for its "main trunk," the association chose well. Poole was well prepared for the responsibility. At Yale, an apprenticeship as assistant librarian of the Brothers Library had been followed by a year in charge of the small but busy library. As a friend of the Yale College librarian, he had become acquainted with the collections and with some of the problems of a larger academic library. From the rich experience of preparing his *Index* he had received an understanding of problems encountered in making catalogs and indexes. The work at the Athenaeum had given him the chance to run the day-to-day operations of a library which was, for its time, very large indeed. Surely there were in 1852 few if any other young men with an equal experience at all levels of library operation. His record was so obviously superior to that of the many other applicants that he was chosen unanimously on the first ballot. The demands and duties of the job were not small. In compensation, Poole was paid $1,000 annually, double the rate of his Athenaeum salary.

The new librarian faced some serious problems. The association occupied quarters that had housed it since 1848. Its needs, including those of the library, had outstripped the available space. Only by periodic sacrifice of other functions was it able to provide for its growing book collection. The two years preceding Poole's appointment had been a time of considerable growth for the library. In 1850, the hours of opening had been extended and a full-time librarian appointed. Having gathered together 7,500 volumes during its thirty years of existence, it added 4,000 more in the next two years. Its printed catalogs had been badly outdistanced by the rapid growth of the collection.

The problems which the association faced were a reflection of its healthy and thriving state, but the difficulties were nonetheless real. Poole accepted his new responsibilities over a collection containing more than 11,000 volumes, including 2,513 added during the previous year at a cost of $2,300. The popular reviews and other magazines were received regularly, as well as newspapers from Boston, New York, Washington, and such distant communities as Pittsburgh and Mobile. The books were selected in accordance with a policy having a two-pronged purpose: to assemble a permanent collection of standard works and classics and to supply the members with the latest popular books. The long-term objective was

that additions should be made to the Library of standard works, of unquestioned merit, in every department of literature and science; that the members may have constant access to all the most approved works, embodying the results of travels and researches of all ages, and of recent scientific experiments and investigations.[2]

To this end also, efforts were made to find volumes to fill gaps in sets of serial publications. Equally, however, the members expected to find enough copies of new books to meet a reasonable proportion of the demands. The association was unusual in its policy of buying many duplicate copies of popular books.

Once acquired, the books were arranged according to arbitrary numbers assigned, with the principal exception of additions to sets, in serial order corresponding to the order of receipt into the collection. As had been true in the Brothers Library, the shelves were closed to all but the librarian and his assistants. The first duty of the librarian, accordingly, was to get the books requested by members. He had then to record the loans in ledgers containing a page for each member.

As the principal full-time employee, Poole was also responsible for overseeing all the operations of the association's quarters and for maintaining order in the rooms. He had to carry on the business affairs connected with acquiring new books and the work of cataloging them. He was required to take care of the multitudinous tasks connected with operating a library, including routine jobs such as putting the books in protective paper covers. He was expected to perform odd jobs, such as keeping an accurate list of the members and notifying them when assessments came due. Since the librarian was the one individual who represented the greatest continuity from year to year, his help was sought in regard to many other recurrent duties that were connected with the library only remotely if at all. The years as a member and an employee of the Brothers in Unity, whose activities and organization paralleled those of the Mercantile Library, gave him a background that especially fitted him to counsel the officers of the association.

Working under the control of these officers and with their close attention, Poole had daily responsibilities in the library and some part in the shaping of policies. Exactly what part he played can be seen only indirectly, and much of his work went unrecorded. It is characteristic of librarianship that much of its work leaves no direct evidence and even indirect testimony and record are sparse. A collection of books, perhaps a building, some reports, catalogs, and correspondence, and a set of dry statistics are the major things a librarian leaves behind him. So it was with Poole. But the signs of accomplishment are plain even in the scanty records that remain.

During Poole's first year, 79,000 books were circulated, about 250 daily, on the average, and 12,000 more than the previous year. At the end of the official year, the officers recorded their satisfaction with Poole's services:

He has been thoroughly educated to his profession, and brings to the discharge of its duties a complete acquaintance with all the practical details in the management of a public library. If the next administration should authorize the publication of a new catalogue of the Library, now so greatly needed by the members, we are confident that his assistance would be invaluable in its preparation.[3]

They gave more concrete evidence of their favor by increasing his salary to the round sum of $100 per month.

Along with his duties at the library, Poole continued to work on the *Index*. Most of the indexing was finished before he went to the Mercantile Library, but some remained to be done. Charles B. Norton, publisher of books and a periodical, *Norton's Literary Gazette and Publishers' Circular,* had announced in 1851 that he would publish the book. Not until March of 1853, however, did printing begin. Norton's sponsorship of the publication was in line with his general interest in bibliography and libraries. Another evidence of that interest was his initiative in organizing a conference of librarians, the first such meeting ever held. When, in September, 1853, the librarians assembled in New York, Poole was among them. At the meeting, most of the attention was given to Charles Coffin Jewett, librarian of the Smithsonian Institution, who described his plans to make it the national library and told the conference about his scheme to prepare library catalogs by means of stereotyped entries made, for the sake of economy, of Indiana clay. Poole later described the plan as "Prof. Jewett's *mud* catalogue" [4] and said it had been his comment at the time. Though Poole warned his listeners years later that many seemingly impractical proposals were later put to use in other connections, it is particularly ironic that this very idea as adapted by Halsey W. Wilson was to drive Poole's own *Index* from the field. In 1853, however, the *Index* was at its beginning, not its end. An advance copy was available for examination at the conference, where a formal resolution of approval was voted. In October, the volume was put on public sale.

The new book was a substantial volume. In contrast to the first edition, it included most of the important periodicals of the time, and it indexed them adequately. Although not reviewed extensively, it was greeted enthusiastically by those journals that mentioned it. The New York *Times* spoke of it as

really a very important book, and we can only wonder how . . . we have managed to do without it. It is henceforth one of the indispensables of student life, a contribution to literature which enforces its own value like an Almanac, a Directory, or a Concordance. . . . Henceforward Mr. Poole's name can never be pronounced without respect.[5]

Despite enthusiastic reviews, the book did not sell rapidly. At $6.00 a copy, it was expensive for that day. Although it probably would have sold out within a few years, Norton's financial difficulties around 1855 forced him to sell the remainder of the 1,000-copy edition at auction, and Poole never received the financial return he had expected from the book. He did benefit, however, from the enhancement of his reputation among librarians and literary men.

With the *Index* completed, Poole soon returned to the preparation of another book to meet the pressing need of his library for a new catalog. To the preparation of this work he brought the bias and background of his experience in compiling the *Index*. It had been solely a subject index, and this emphasis on the subject approach led Poole rather naturally to the plan that produced a new kind of library catalog.

The catalogs of the time were of two main types. The classic form was a subject catalog, often including a separate author index. But the difficulties and complexities of such so-called systematic catalogs for both maker and user had impelled many librarians to choose rather to prepare a list of books arranged alphabetically by author. These author catalogs took many forms. Some were elaborate and detailed lists with full bibliographical descriptions and notes as well as a careful subject index. Others were brief author lists. The evolution from the pure author catalog to the full dictionary catalog was natural and reasonable, though not so rational nor so orderly in its development as the following diagrammatic description might seem to imply. The maker of an author list met with a problem when he had to list an anonymous work; the necessity for finding a proper entry led logically to the use of a title entry in these cases. Once some titles had been introduced, it was an easy step to the inclusion of full title lists within the alphabet. But, if titles were to be included, it seemed only sensible to select for the entry not necessarily the first but rather the most significant and easily remembered word of the title. This so-called catchword title was seen to have a value for finding books from the point of view of their subjects. And some librarians, more concerned with practicality than with logic and consistency, began to interject a few pure subject entries. The further step to the inclusion of subject entries for all books, other than works of fiction, was a natural outgrowth of the previous developments, but it was a step which no one before Poole had taken.

Though the development of the complete dictionary catalog

was evolutionary and gradual, it was not inevitable that the 1854 catalog of the Mercantile Library Association of Boston should be the one to represent the last step. This result came about both because the time was ripe for it and because a person of Poole's background was in the key position at the moment. He knew that an entry by author was essential in a circulating library. Knowing that readers were often ignorant of authors' names, he concluded that title entries too were indispensable. The experience with the *Index* made him tend toward a comprehensive inclusion of subject entries. The form of the *Index* and its frequent comparison to a dictionary inclined him toward that plan for the catalog. In total, the catalog he produced reflected an approach emphasizing the practical and the instrumental rather than the logical and the theoretical. The catalog was a working tool to serve the specific purpose of helping readers to find the books they wanted. It had no other purpose, and it was not complicated by the inclusion of features other than those which were thought to serve the single end.

The sort of catalog chosen had merit not only because the final product achieved the purpose for which it was designed but also because it could be prepared more quickly and easily than could other, more complicated types. With only a single alphabetical list of authors, titles, and subjects to make, Poole was not faced with the necessity to coordinate two or more different parts, as was true of makers of classed catalogs or of author catalogs with subject indexes. A maker of the latter type, for example, had to wait until the author list was finished before he could complete the subject index by inserting page or entry numbers.

The whole process, direct though it was, was completed by Poole in a phenomenally short time. Hardly more than six months elapsed between the authorization of the catalog and its delivery for sale in the library on November 10, 1854. Although the association by that time had employed an assistant librarian and, during the preparation of the catalog, had allowed the hiring of an additional temporary assistant, Poole had to do the job while still carrying the responsibility of librarian of the association. The simplicity of the plan made the task an uncomplicated one, but it was Poole's energy and diligence that enabled him to complete it so quickly.

The new volume was later described by Charles Ammi Cutter as "the first complete triple asyndetic dictionary catalogue." [6] Actually, it was not precisely a dictionary catalog in the later sense of the term. It did contain author, title, and subject entries, but in most cases the subject entries were really catchword titles. There was, except for works of fiction, no complete listing of all titles by the first word which was not an article. The book was a mixture of entries for authors, pure subjects, catchword titles, and pure titles. Nor was it totally "asyndetic," for some cross references did appear. They were all "see" references simply indicating the term used under a term not used—for example, "Bonaparte, *see* Napoleon." There were no "see also" references to lead the reader from one subject to another. There was, in fact, no orderly plan of cross references or subject headings. Poole followed his practice in making the *Index* by limiting himself almost exclusively to the wording of the book title. And, with the *Catalogue,* as with the *Index,* this limitation appreciably reduced the difficulty of the job. It meant also, however, that books on the same subject might be separated widely in the alphabet by the accident of word choice. But, in sum, the catalog was a practical kind of instrument for the ordinary circulating libraries of the time. Some twenty years later, Cutter gave his informed judgment on the merits and influence of the form introduced by Poole: "From its economy of space, its facility of use, the ease with which any one who can copy accurately can make it, and its apparent completeness, it has been a favorite type with town and mercantile libraries." [7]

The preparation of the catalog had not occupied Poole's exclusive attention. Presumably, some of his time during those months was spent in calling on Miss Fanny Maria Gleason, daughter of Dr. Ezra W. Gleason. Poole waited until after the completion of the catalog to take an important step in his personal life; on November 22, 1854, twelve days after the catalog was put on sale in the library, he was married to the young lady. She was then twenty years old and he not quite thirty-three.

Poole's success in preparing the catalog had not been matched by a general prosperity of the association as a whole, but the library's condition was excellent. The whole collection had been refurbished. Poole and his helpers had taken advantage of the necessity of handling each book during cataloging to make repairs, to put each volume in a paper cover, to discard or replace worn or missing copies, and to acquire books needed to fill in gaps. As a result, the library was "probably never in so good order as at present." In that condition, it was "believed not to be surpassed in value by any library of its size in the country." [8]

Good as was the condition of the library, its use had declined as a result of a loss of membership in the association. Various competing groups had sprung up in Boston to draw off some of the members. The most damaging of these agencies was the new public library, which had opened its doors for the circulation of books on May 2, 1854. Its initial 12,000 volumes had been increased in less than a year to more than 19,000, making its collection immediately larger than that assembled in the Mercantile Library during a quarter of a century. A free institution open to all over the age of twenty-one, the public library naturally had lured a number of members away from the association. Although some of the defectors returned after finding the services of the public library less satisfactory for their needs, a number continued to prefer a free institution.

The rivalry of the new library did not discourage the officers of the association. Instead, in a remarkable burst of energy, they responded to the challenge by obtaining handsome new quarters and expanding their services. The moves were successful in raising the membership to record levels, but they also made the association vulnerable if membership should decline so far that it could no longer support the cost of services. With the coming of a new, timid administration, the feared decline did occur, and, though the association survived for a number of years longer, it finally gave up the struggle in 1877, turning over its books to the public library and remaining in existence only as a social club. The competition of a free public library was too much for most of the vocational libraries of the nineteenth century, and so it was for the Mercantile Library Association of Boston.

Poole did not remain to see the gradual decline of the associa-

The Pooles with Their Twin Daughters Helen and Alice, about 1856

tion. Early in April of 1856, Charles Folsom resigned as librarian of the Athenaeum, and, on the 28th of the same month, the trustees elected Poole to the position. In making the decision to leave the Mercantile Library, Poole did not require long deliberation. His letter of resignation cited "the increase of salary, the small number of hours of daily labor, and the enlarged facilities for perfecting myself in the higher branches of my profession." [9] The Athenaeum was one of the largest libraries in the country. Its librarianship promised opportunities for a lifetime of work. The scope for advancement and the prestige of the position could not have been scorned by any ambitious man. And Poole had special reason to seek advancement, for, in September of 1855, he had become the father of twins, Alice and Helen.

The officers of the Mercantile Library were sorry to see him go:

This gentleman, who has occupied the office of Librarian for nearly four years, with eminent ability and success, and whose influence during that time, happily for us, has extended beyond the mere routine of the immediate duties of his office, was a few weeks since elected Librarian of the Boston Athenaeum—a situation more worthy of his talents and superior qualifications than we had it in our power to offer him.

He carries with him our warmest wishes for his success in life, and our sincere thanks for all the numerous services, not strictly in the line of his duties, which he has so freely and so kindly rendered us. His services during the past year have been as valuable and as acceptable as in any of the preceding years he has been associated with us, and this is as high commendation as we can give.[10]

With the consciousness of approval from his associates, Poole went to the Athenaeum to take up new responsibilities.

III. The Boston Athenaeum, 1856-1868

The Boston Athenaeum had a long and proud history extending back to its origins in the Anthology Society in 1805. It had become a proprietary institution in 1807 under a charter from the Massachusetts legislature, with membership based on the ownership of shares. By 1856, there were about a thousand shares in the hands of its aristocratic proprietors. Its total assets were valued at half a million dollars and included art works, a substantial three-story building, and a collection of 60,000 books described as "hardly surpassed, either in size or in value, by any other in the country." [1]

The fine collection included a part of George Washington's private library, which had been bought in 1848 by a group of leading citizens for presentation to the Athenaeum. Also particularly prized were the transactions of the leading European learned societies, the great encyclopedias, Buffon's *Natural History*, the architect Piranesi's works in twenty-nine folio volumes, Gould's magnificent *Birds of Europe*, and many other works of similar importance. The Athenaeum had grown into an excellent library, much of it purchased after careful and informed selection. Its collection was one of the largest in the nation. Its sheltered position, the scholarly interests of its users, and the wealth of its financial resources had ensured the purchase or donation of many valuable and important books.

Poole thus entered a library not merely four times larger than the Mercantile Library but many times richer in the quality of its book collection. Here was no bustling reading room with a desk dispensing several hundred popular novels each day—the Athenaeum's annual circulation was less than 14,000. It was in the Athenaeum that Hildreth had composed much of his *History of the United States*. Emerson and Oliver Wendell Holmes would be likely to come in to borrow volumes to satisfy their omnivorous reading tastes. George Ticknor or Edward Everett might drop by to examine some book not in his own fine private collection. The atmosphere was one of quiet reading, if not always of study and research.

The resources which had made possible the creation of such a library were very large. The Athenaeum's assets included special funds used solely for the purchase of books; the Bromfield Fund of some $29,000 and the Appleton Fund rated at $25,000 brought in a substantial income each year. The wealth of the Athenaeum was a decisive factor in enabling the institution to survive while many similar societies were dying or being swallowed up by publicly supported libraries.

In so conservative an institution, the young man of thirty-four found it less easy to make an impression than he had in the Mercantile Library, where his patrons were perpetually youthful, untried, eager, and progressive. Nevertheless, he appeared regularly in the library, giving attention to his own duties and supervising the work of his staff. He made recommendations to the Library Committee for the adaptation of services and facilities to changing conditions. He took a personal hand in the daily operations, with the result that the orderliness of the collection and its quarters improved. He took an active part in the selection, location, and acquisition of new resources. He made his presence felt.

The Athenaeum, in turn, had its effect on him. The years at Yale and at the Mercantile Library had given him valuable experience in the practical management of library affairs, but their collections had been devoted to works of popular reading. At the Athenaeum, he was for the first time in charge of a scholarly library. He had the opportunity to broaden his knowledge of rare books, standard literature, and bibliography. He associated with many of the leading writers of American literature and history and did some writing of his own in these fields. His place at the Athenaeum gave him prestige and standing among the colleagues of his profession. And, in the shelter of his position, his family grew and matured.

There were problems in the library which Poole had to face at once. In one of his first official acts, he proposed a rearrangement of the books to provide more space and a better system of classification. Complete and perfect subject classification of a large library, he said in a report to the Library Committee, was neither practical nor even possible. With his characteristic dependence on the titles of books as an index to their subject content, he pointed out the ambiguity of many titles and the varied subject nature of many individual books. Even if these difficulties did not stand in the way, complete shelf classification would be defeated by the many different sizes of books on the same subject. Here Poole expressed the conclusion to which he held throughout his life: "A proximate classification is all that can be accomplished." Nor was it necessary to have the various classes "follow each other in that logical sequence which their scientific relations to each other would seem to require in a perfect classification by subjects. General convenience of reference and sightly appearance of the rooms" were more important than precisely logical relationships. But, even though imperfect, a subject arrangement, he said, "is of great importance in a reference library and can be easily secured." [2]

The call numbers of the books were closely tied to the numbering of the shelves. The library contained twenty-six alcoves, each designated by a different letter of the alphabet. Each alcove was supposed to contain ten tiers of shelves, each tier ten shelves high. Thus, a simple numerical system could denote any individual shelf in the library. For example, G43 would mean alcove G, tier 4, shelf 3. The individual books were not given distinctive numbers other than those assigning them to a particular shelf. By designating certain alcoves to contain specific subjects, a kind of subject classification was obtained, though it was certainly "proximate."

Poole was advocating a rearrangement of the library, not a complete reclassification. He proposed to make adjustments in a general plan already in existence. The subjects used were very broad, were often based on considerations other than the substantive content of the books, and were designed to fit the particular collection rather than to provide a systematic plan for the whole of knowledge. Some of the classes were pure subjects and were subdivided in conventional ways. History, Poole proposed, would be broken down by period, by geography, and by degree of generality. First would be General Works; then Ancient History, divided into

General Works, Greece, and Rome; then the Middle Ages; then the histories of individual countries arranged under the continents —Europe, Asia, Africa, and America. Under the United States would be places for state histories and then for town histories. Specific though this plan might be, it was still rather broadly and casually defined. Another ostensible subject, Periodical Works, was really a class based on form of publication. Still another, Bibliography, was also a division based on form, as well as on the use expected for the books in it. There were classes by type rather than subject, such as Guidebooks, Fiction, and Statistics. Slavery, a subject of great current interest and much writing, was set up as a separate class rather than in a logical relationship with broader subjects. Poole was not hampered by any qualms about violating a logical sequence of classification when he proposed the establishment of a new subdivision for School Books.

The difficulties with the classification lay not in its lack of a theoretical base or of close subdivision but rather in the notation, which provided for a form of fixed location. The result of this system was to require changes in call numbers each time the collection was shifted. Although it is difficult enough to foresee the requirements for expansion with a notation that provides for relative location, fixed location urgently requires that room for growth be provided within each subject class and even within each subdivision. Failure to do so at the Athenaeum meant inevitably that frequent moves and new call numbers would be required. In the meantime, the shelves would become so crowded that books would have to be stored in double rows, one behind the other. Some time later, Poole proposed to solve this problem by the construction of a series of internal staircases to provide access to the rooms above and below the library, all under the control of the attendant at the sole entrance to the library on the middle floor. This ingenious plan, however, the trustees did not put into effect until years later, when the need for large amounts of new space could no longer be denied. The policy of delaying the provision of new space until the need proved desperate meant that staff time was wasted in frequent shifts of books and that the collection was chronically crowded. Since only a little extra space was provided with each move, Poole had to do the best he could to predict the critical areas of pressure and had to look forward to another rearrangement soon. This difficulty was especially troublesome because he was, at the same time, embarking on the preparation of a new printed catalog which, if it contained outmoded shelf marks, would cause serious inconvenience.

A new catalog was badly needed. The last full listing of the collection had been published in 1827, when the library had contained fewer than 16,000 volumes. Supplements had been issued in 1830, 1833, and 1840, but nothing further had been published in the ensuing sixteen years while the collection had grown from 31,000 volumes to twice that size. The only complete record was to be found in a crude card file at the circulation desk. The cards had been prepared by many hands over a number of years, so that they varied greatly in consistency and accuracy. They were inconvenient to use and could not easily be made available to the patrons. Having completed his Mercantile Library catalog quickly, Poole expected to produce a similar one readily for the Athenaeum, though the larger size of the collection meant that the project would take longer. This work was not to take the place of the card catalog, which, though imperfect, was designed to provide full descriptive cataloging. The new catalog was to be prepared in addition to the card catalog as a way to meet the reader's needs quickly and easily.

With a new catalog to prepare, Poole needed an enlarged staff. Up to that time, the staff consisted simply of the librarian and an assistant librarian. Poole's first assistant librarian was a young newspaperman who soon returned to journalism and was replaced by a former school principal whose health had not been up to the requirements of his school duties. Library jobs in the nineteenth century were considered suitable stopgaps for those who, for one reason or another, could not find other employment. Poole was a rarity in having made a deliberate decision to be a librarian. The Athenaeum soon took a brave step in hiring another of the marginally employable in the person of Mrs. A. B. Harnden, who may have been the first woman to be employed in an American library. This action flew in the face of a warning by Poole's predecessor that the presence of women in a library containing examples of "the corrupter portions of the polite literature" would cause "frequent embarrassment to modest men." [3] Once the door was opened, the men of the Athenaeum evidently became lost to social delicacy, for Mrs. Harnden was only the first of a long series of female employees.

In supervising the staff, Poole's way was "to set them at a task with a fair amount of instruction, and then leave them to show what was in them." [4] He coupled this implied confidence in his assistants with a personal interest in each of them, and he allowed them to see in him the standards of conduct and values to which he adhered. One day in the library he told how, on the previous evening, he had taken the opportunity offered by a chance meeting with Wendell Phillips to correct an inaccurate story which Phillips had been including in his public lectures. That night in Melrose, when Phillips told the original version without change, Poole was less outraged than amazed at what he considered such total lack of integrity. By revealing himself thus to his subordinates and by showing interest and confidence in them, Poole built up a remarkable sense of loyalty and affection in a notable roster of his employees who went on to attain distinction. William Isaac Fletcher, perhaps his most faithful disciple, told of one instance when Poole's effort to demonstrate the proper methods to him ended in chagrin. Poole was quite sure of the correct way to dust books. Never, he said, should anyone try to dust with a cloth, because the attempt only forced the dirt into the leaves and smeared the edges. The right way was to take two books of equal size and to strike them together smartly, thus dislodging the dust and leaving the books clean and bright. As Fletcher told it,

I was one day making awkward work of slapping together some large quartos when Mr. Poole came along and undertook to give me a demonstration. He brought two volumes together with a good whack, but as they did not meet quite fairly they caromed on each other and slid far across the floor in either direction. I was speedily left to my own devices! [5]

But even the embarrassing moments added a touch of humanity to the impression which his subordinates got from Poole.

His tolerant attitude did not always produce the necessary accuracy and speed in the work. Poole had never before been in a position that required any substantial delegation of responsibility, and he did not always recognize adequately the importance of keeping in close touch with the work that his subordinates were doing. Larger libraries, like the Athenaeum, were beginning to require more staff members than the one or two who had been sufficient up to that time. Those librarians, like Poole, who had been accustomed to participating closely in all aspects of library operation had to learn skills of staff management and supervision.

Projects such as a rearrangement or a new catalog of the collection had to be done in addition to the regular work of the library. Although the assistant librarian probably had to care for the charging desk initially, it was not long before the employment of new assistants made it possible for him to turn over that routine duty to others. The desk attendant was responsible for maintaining the ledger where book charges were recorded and, on request, for finding books on the shelves. Usually, in the open-shelf collection, the patron got his own books and, if he wished to take them home, brought them to the desk to be charged to him. At a corner of the library overlooking the circulation desk, Poole performed his own duties, which included ordering new books, a responsibility that he shared with the assistant librarian. When the books arrived, the janitors unpacked them and gave them to the desk attendant, whose job was to collate them, cut the leaves, and emboss the library's stamp on the title pages. The assistant librarian then noted them in the accession book. After that, the books were ready to be cataloged and entered in the shelf list, which was used as the basis for the inventory taken during the annual closing.

The Athenaeum had been fortunate to find so readily a man like Poole who could take immediate hold of his job both as to detail and as to policy. In his approach to his work, Poole represented a significant change from his predecessor, Charles Folsom, who had concerned himself less with the details of daily operations than with the duties of helping the patrons to find what they wanted. Folsom's intimate knowledge of the collection was in line with the bent of his own predecessor, William Smith Shaw, who had made the Athenaeum his very life. These men belonged to an older tradition of librarian, the modern concept of which is a musty antiquarian devoted to his books, although the inference that he tried to prevent rather than to foster their use would appear to be a slander against many of the breed. For them the daily administration of a library was an annoying triviality of their careers, to be performed with the least possible trouble.

Poole, on the other hand, was of a newer generation of librarian. To these men also, books and bibliography were important aspects of their work, but all too often that side of librarianship had to bow to the practical necessities of finding space for the volumes and carrying on the daily business of building a collection and providing for its housing and care. The collection at the Athenaeum was reaching a size that was difficult for a librarian to know intimately or to care for personally without a growing staff of assistants.

Poole's work earned him the approval of the trustees at the end of his first year, as it did throughout his tenure. The secretary commented: "He has administrative qualities that are valuable to the Athenaeum. He is prompt, accurate and economical and to my mind the business of the institution is better conducted than it has been formerly." [6]

Poole's attention to administrative matters did not mean neglect of the bibliographical side of his job. He acted as the Athenaeum's agent in significant ways in selecting books to be acquired, in buying from book stores, and in bidding at auctions. When, during the Civil War, the Athenaeum's resources for buying exceeded the number of books readily available for purchase, he went to the bookstores of New York and Philadelphia to compile lists of titles from which the trustees could select. Not infrequently, he went to New York to represent the Athenaeum at auctions, and, on one notable occasion, he went as far as Washington to bid on a group of books purporting to be from the first President's library. Poole was one of the knowledgeable buyers who immediately detected the bookplates as forgeries, but, since the Athenaeum had a special interest in Washingtoniana, he bought a number of books as curiosities. The fact that Poole was repeatedly the Athenaeum's representative at auctions demonstrates his skill, for the bookish patrons and trustees would have been quick to detect a bad blunder.

During the Civil War, Poole was active in seeking the publications of the Confederacy for his library. When, at the close of hostilities, it became possible to buy in the former rebel territories, he embarked on a vigorous campaign to make the Athenaeum's collection of Confederate publications pre-eminent in the nation. One notable opportunity came when historian Francis Parkman, at the time a member of the Library Committee, decided to visit Richmond and the Virginia battlefields. He was authorized to spend $500 for important books, pamphlets, and newspapers. Poole kept in touch with him by letter, advising him on prices, people to see, and the special needs of the library. The collecting effort was not confined to such special opportunities but involved a wide net of correspondents throughout the South, with Poole directing the activities of some and soliciting the aid of others. This buying program had the objective of making "for the Athenaeum (for the benefit of future historians) a very complete collection of newspapers, pamphlets, books and documents of every description printed at the South during the rebellion." To this end, *"Nothing printed* is too trivial to fall beneath the dignity of our undertaking. Almanacs, song-books, circulars, story-books, whatever goes to illustrate the condition and action of the Southern mind comes within our plan." This was no selfish, local interest. Poole wrote:

It is as broad as the country. Whatever we collect will be sacredly kept for the benefit of whoever has occasion to consult [it], whether he be a resident of Mass. or Tennessee. We have undertaken it because it requires a considerable outlay of means, and our procuring means are larger than most of the libraries in the country. We are putting our energies and money into it, while the ephemeral publications of the South can be procured.[7]

By vigorous pursuit of this goal, not without competition, the Athenaeum soon could be said to have the largest collection of Confederate literature in the North. Its very size and richness became a magnet for gifts of similar material, and Poole felt justified in claiming the right to buy from a smaller library under his modification of Scripture: "Unto him that hath shall be *sold.*" [8] The result of this campaign was to make the Athenaeum's Confederate collection the best in the country.

The work on the catalog which was to record all the new acquisitions was less successful. The original plan was that Poole and the assistant librarian, with special assistance, would do the work.

For some reason, probably associated more with the administration and service of the library than with the catalog itself, he seems never to have become closely involved with the cataloging. Early in the project, Charles Russell Lowell, brother of the poet, was employed as one of the workers and became the one person whose work covered virtually all the years of the catalog's production. Lowell was a gentle, conscientious soul, whose ideal for the catalog was perfection. Nothing could have been further from Poole's plans, for his method was to produce such a work as quickly as possible so that it could become a useful tool of service. A careful bibliographical and descriptive catalog was not, in his view, an appropriate production to meet the needs of the Athenaeum. This conflict of understanding, coupled with Poole's way of letting a subordinate work without close supervision, meant that the catalog took a direction which was both unexpected and unwanted. The pursuit of perfection so slowed the work that no catalog was printed during Poole's tenure.

The failure to produce the catalog was caused partly by the substantial number of acquisitions each year, complicated by frequent shifts of the book collection and consequent changes of shelf marks. More fundamentally, the failure was rooted in four primary factors: library techniques that, though in the main as advanced as those in general use, were crude and primitive by modern standards; Poole's failure to recognize the importance of specifying uniform rules and ensuring adherence to them; Lowell's perfectionism; and, most important, the confused and ill-defined administrative organization of the institution.

One of these factors, although perhaps the least important, was the primitive system of book notation which, by a modified form of fixed location, tied the books to the shelves and made it necessary to change the call numbers each time the books were moved. Poole saw this difficulty and warned of it regularly, but the only solution he had to suggest was to provide enough extra space so that moves would be necessary only at long intervals. He did not realize that a more fundamental solution would be to devise a notation that was independent of the shelves. But to charge him with failure on this account would be much too harsh; notation schemes that provided for relative rather than fixed location were a later development. He was, after all, William Frederick Poole; it would be unreasonable to expect him to have been Melvil Dewey as well. Since the trustees did not provide large enough blocks of space at any one time, the years between 1856 and 1869 were filled with frequent shifts in the collection. Each move meant the preparation of new shelf lists, renumbering of the books, and further delay of the catalog.

The second major difficulty was Poole's blindness to the need for standardization as the heavy burden of library work began to demand that more than one person be employed on the catalog. He failed to provide detailed and specific directions to guide the catalogers, and he did not supervise the work closely enough to be aware of the kind of cataloging that was being done. Having prepared indexes and a catalog himself without written rules or established subject-heading lists, he thought he could trust the common sense and intelligence of those doing the work. What he did not see was that uniformity, consistency, and completeness could be obtained only if the rules of entry, the details of description, and the wording of subjects were carefully spelled out. He thought that anyone should know, after brief instruction, how to index a periodical or catalog a book. He did not realize that one person's judgment on such matters might be very different from another's or that even the same person's decisions might be made on different bases from time to time. He did not take adequately into account the fact that a set of specific rules and a standard list of subject headings could have made the work consistent. Formal subject-heading lists did not become an accepted feature of library operation for some years, but there were published rules of entry and description, one set prepared by Poole's acquaintance, Charles Coffin Jewett. This leader of the library world had even recognized the necessity for subject-heading lists and had expressed the hope of preparing one, but this was only a gleam in his eye; the rules were an actuality of which Poole took inadequate account. No doubt he would have rejected as unsuitable the kind of full cataloging called for in Jewett's rules, but nothing prevented him from adapting them as he thought best or, in lieu of that, writing new ones. And to try to make a catalog using a number of different workers without explicit rules was foolhardy. The attempt produced the kind of chaotic catalog that Jewett had warned, with graphic illustrations, would come from working without rules.

The lack of detailed rules did not mean that Poole gave no instructions to the catalogers. The work which they produced bore his own special stamp in the close conformity of the subject wording to the language of the book titles. It is likely that the instructions he gave were as informal and general as those which he detailed some twenty years later to the contributors to the third edition of the *Index*.

Abridge the title when it is practicable, so that the entire reference will come in a single line. . . . If the indexer finds that he cannot write on every line, or cannot bring his references, as a rule, into a single line, he may be sure that his handwriting or his skill in abridging titles is not up to the standard of the model indexer.[9]

If the directions were as vague as these, it is not surprising that the results failed to satisfy the exacting standards of a dedicated cataloger like Charles Ammi Cutter, the man who eventually published the catalog begun in 1856. Titles were abbreviated and inverted. Anonymous and pseudonymous works were entered without extensive research into authorship. When an author's name was given in a book, it was accepted without verification and without the addition of dates of birth and death. Reliance upon the wording of titles as a guide to subject content produced some ludicrously mistaken subject entries, particularly for books in foreign languages. The facts of publication were not meticulously determined and listed. Catalog entries with defects like these could be brought together into a single work and could even be substantially improved by a vigorous and knowledgeable person with the capacity to finish the less-than-perfect. Poole proved both before and after that time that he had that capacity. There can be no real doubt that he could have finished the Athenaeum catalog. Indeed, in the fact that the catalog was reported to be complete at the end of 1860 and again at the end of 1861, there is some reason to believe that he actually did take supervisory hold of the work himself. But the trustees could not see their way clear to allow the printing to proceed and, in fact, formally gave over the direction of the work to Lowell. After that time, Poole had virtually no connection with the project. This action of the trustees was a mistake. In thinking that Lowell could complete the job, they misjudged their man.

Charles Russell Lowell was a devoted and conscientious worker, but he knew little of system and less of administration. He was full of excuses. He could blame his troubles on the work done before he took charge of the catalog without once mentioning that he had been the first to be employed as a cataloger and the one person who had been occupied with the work throughout the years. He was the kind of man who, after at least three years in full charge, could report the catalog as complete and then could spend almost five years more in making corrections, without finishing them. It was this perfectionist who kept constantly raising the standards until the objective had become the production of a bibliographical catalog. And in the words of a committee of the trustees, "a Bibliographical Catalogue of such a library as ours, is, as every one sees, a work of time, of almost indefinite time." [10]

In a properly organized library no tenderness for a faithful employee's feelings would have been allowed to frustrate the institution's objectives. But the Athenaeum's organization was both unwise and confused. The board was jealous of its authority, delegating it only as far as its own committees. The Standing Committee, though subject to review by the board, had absolute power over daily affairs and was expected to exercise close control. The Library Committee, too, dealt with the minutest matters at its frequent meetings. Far from having both the authority and the responsibility for the library and its employees, the librarian was not allowed "to have the entire direction and parcelling out of the work." The trustees had "settled the matter at the Athenaeum and fixed the employments of each person." [11] Neither the trustees nor their committees had any hesitancy about dabbling in any phase of library operations without reference to the librarian. This failure to put both responsibility and authority wholly in Poole's hands without bypassing or undercutting him cost the Athenaeum dearly. With firm support from the trustees, he could have saved the situation; as it was, the project was taken away from him entirely. In a modern library organization, he would be held to blame for letting the affair go on so long. As matters were arranged at the Athenaeum, however, he cannot be held responsible for the long-range delay. No one at the Athenaeum did blame him nor did he make any effort to defend himself. It must have been very clear to all that the catalog was neither his province nor his responsibility.

Many years later, Fletcher made a statement that stands as a fair summary of the catalog, the course of the work on it, and its final end.

There is no more interesting and instructive chapter in American library history than that of this Boston Athenaeum catalog; of how it was subjected to higher and ever higher standards of thoroughness and excellence, and finally appeared, under the admirable editorship of Mr. Charles A. Cutter, who had succeeded Mr. Poole, in 1872–82, in five large volumes, a genuine marvel of fulness, accuracy, and bibliographical scholarship. The story is pretty fully told in the note appended to the last volume of the catalog; but with all its financial implications, it never has been and probably will not be. The expense, beyond what it would have cost to make and keep up a first-rate catalog, was, from first to last, enormous, nor can it reasonably be justified on any pretense of a commensurate advantage to the library or its users. It is a monumental achievement in bibliography, and has been, as it always will be, of great use to other libraries and to individuals outside, but for the Athenaeum itself it was decidedly a losing venture.[12]

Large plans and projects were the matters on the surface of events, but Poole's work at the Athenaeum was composed mainly of the small routines and actions that came up from day to day. He supervised the work of a staff which grew over the years from one assistant and two janitors to seven assistants and one janitor. He himself handled many of the minor tasks, writing to a supplier about a ten-cent error on a bill or to a binder about poor work received in a shipment and personally taking apart a rare book, repairing its leaves, and rebinding it. Except when away on business or vacation, he was in the library each day, even coming in at times on holidays to take advantage of the chance to work quietly. His work, both in large matters and in detail, satisfied the trustees. Not free with praise, they nevertheless expressed their pleasure from time to time and, more significantly, relied upon him for advice and allowed him to speak and act on the Athenaeum's behalf. Concretely, they rewarded his services by increases in salary from $1,200 to $1,500 in 1858, to $2,000 in 1865, and to $2,500 in 1867.

Poole's feeling of satisfaction from his work at the Athenaeum was reinforced by other pleasures. At his home in Melrose, he became a part of the community, making warm friends, among whom were banker Elbridge H. Goss, best known as the author of a well-regarded biography of Paul Revere, and Daniel Gooch, the local Congressman. Poole was one of the founders and a vice-president of the local Young Men's Christian Association and vice-president of the Union League, as well as the organizer of an appeal for funds for the relief of the families of local servicemen. He himself, though an ardent Union supporter, was never seriously in peril of being called to service, but he joined a local rifle club where he became an expert sharpshooter. As a man of almost forty with a family, he was only marginally eligible for the draft. By 1862, he had four daughters, despite the death in 1856 of one of the first-born twins.

With four little girls, his family life could hardly have been quiet and uneventful, but he continued his habit of devoting his evenings to writing or indexing. Much of the work on the first two editions of the *Index* was done at night. Not long after his 1853 edition was published, he found a new outlet for his energies in the *Mercantile Library Reporter*. He advised the editors and wrote articles for publication in that journal. Some dealt with the library; others were reports of the association's public lectures; and still others were concerned with general literary subjects. In one of his pieces, published in 1855 under the title "Battle of the Dictionaries," he sought to refute the common assertion that Worcester's dictionary was more popular in Boston than was its great rival which bore the name of Noah Webster. The relative amount of use of the two works in the Mercantile Library and in the Athenaeum, he said, justified quite the opposite conclusion.

Poole's article so pleased the Merriams, publishers of the Webster dictionary, that they printed it as a separate in 1856. Then, in 1857, his *Websterian Orthography; a Reply to Dr. Noah Webster's Calumniators* was published in Boston, and, in 1859, *The Orthographical Hobgoblin* was issued from the dictionary's home base of Springfield, Massachusetts. The Merriams were obliged to maintain their own side in the controversy, but it was a duty that delighted them. The argument over the relative merits of the differing forms of spelling and definition generated not simply heat but also substantial sales for the dictionary. If the Merriams could stir things up by printing a few pamphlets, they were glad to do so.

Poole's other writings did not mean that he had abandoned indexing. He continued to hope that an edition of the *Index* would pay, and he worked at intervals on a new manuscript up into the 1870s. In 1863, it was announced that he would publish a new edition covering periodicals to the end of that year and that henceforth periodic supplements would keep the work up to date. Although no book was produced for twenty years, indexing was an activity to which he devoted himself, with some interruptions, for most of the rest of his life.

In 1865 and 1866, Poole's indexing work was interrupted by a venture into historical writing. He undertook to prepare a new edition of an important early New England history. Edward Johnson's *Wonder-Working Providence of Sion's Saviour in New England* was, like the histories of Governor Winthrop and Governor Bradford, a chronicle of the pioneer days of Massachusetts. It had the special merit of being the work of one who, while active in public affairs, was closer to the life of the people than were the two governors. Originally published in the seventeenth century, the work did not exist in a satisfactory edition for nineteenth-century students. Poole decided to issue a facsimile of the original together with an extended introduction and—a book by Poole had to have one—a new index.

The work involved considerable research into manuscript sources and other historical documents. Most important in connection with his profession, Poole undertook some highly sophisticated bibliographical investigations. By evidence of peculiarities of type face and numbering of signatures, he proved that two parts of a certain composite book were not, in fact, two different printing jobs, but one. Since they were one and followed each other directly, it was not possible that a certain introduction was misplaced in binding as scholars had previously maintained. The application of a knowledge of printing techniques to problems of bibliography was not unknown in Poole's day, but its use in historical or literary criticism was most uncommon. When, some forty years later, Shakespearean bibliographers used these methods in their studies, they were considered pioneers.

The new book was a credit to the Athenaeum's librarian and to the institution he served. The research had been careful and extensive. In making catalogs and indexes, Poole advocated finishing a work in time to be useful even if imperfect, but, in writing about historical or bibliographical matters, he believed in precise and accurate statement. He might misread his evidence, he might state a conclusion more positively than others would think warranted, he might be wrong in his interpretations, but he was not one to say inadvertently something he did not mean nor to fail from lack of hard work to find relevant evidence.

The book was not Poole's only writing at the time. He became involved in historical debate over some of the issues raised by his study of Johnson's book and eventually gathered his own and his opponents' newspaper articles in a published volume with an extended bibliography that he had prepared. He reviewed a reprint of Anne Bradstreet's poetry in the *North American Review*. Over the years he also reviewed books for the Boston newspapers. All of these writings helped his reputation as the Athenaeum's librarian and gave him first-hand knowledge of the bibliographical needs of scholars.

In another outside venture, he served from 1858 to 1870 as a member of the Visiting Committee for the Harvard Library and, in 1862, wrote its report, in which he advocated public exposure and punishment for petty pilferers of libraries. In the same report, he urged that Harvard's "alphabetico-classed" subject catalog be changed to a strictly alphabetical one. Harvard's system arranged broad subjects alphabetically but with detailed logical subdivision under each topic. Poole pointed out the fact that such a plan required of the catalog's user considerable knowledge of subject relationships. Moreover, it scattered references to a single subject, such as Tobacco, under broad headings depending upon its application: cultivation under Agriculture, effects on human beings under Physiology, and ethics of use under Philosophy. The next year, Harvard's associate librarian, Ezra Abbot, replied showing that Poole's plan would destroy the unity and completeness of references under the broad subjects Agriculture, Physiology, and Philosophy. The subject of this debate was to remain an important topic of controversy among librarians. Though the champions of the classed catalog were never wholly routed, the alphabetical plan was the one eventually adopted by most American libraries.

By 1868, Poole had served twelve years as the Athenaeum's librarian. His stature in the world of libraries and scholarship had increased. His position might have been considered an enviable one, but, in a puzzling move, he wrote a letter to the chairman of the Library Committee expressing his wish to leave office "as soon as I can make other arrangements for future employment, which I have now in contemplation." [13]

One Poole biographer, Carl B. Roden, has suggested that the explanation for Poole's resignation may be found in the fact that Charles Coffin Jewett had died on January 8, 1868, leaving vacant the superintendency of the Boston Public Library. Remembering that Poole had considered seeking the post of librarian there in 1852, Roden speculated that the resignation was a maneuver intended to emphasize Poole's availability for the appointment. The explanation seems unlikely. Ten days after Poole's resignation, Justin Winsor was named superintendent at a salary $500 less than Poole's Athenaeum salary. Moreover, Poole remained at his post for ten months more, and he was replaced only after he had made a second, urgent request to the board. Another event early in 1868 was very close to Poole and may well have been at the base of his determination to leave the Athenaeum.[14]

On January 14, William Frederick Poole, Jr., was born. He was the Pooles' seventh and last child and their first boy. Four of the little girls had survived, but now, in realization of a fond hope of any man, Poole had a son. It was enough to make him stop to consider seriously his life and his prospects. He was forty-six years old. After twelve years at the Athenaeum, he may have become stale and bored with the job, as his recent preoccupation with historical and bibliographical writing might indicate. Although his salary had been raised over the years, he could have had little prospect of a substantial improvement financially at the Athenaeum. In this situation and with the special spur of a newborn son, it would not have been strange for a man of courage to decide to strike out boldly. His new resolve went much deeper than any chance event of the moment.

Poole's resignation came only as a prelude to a busy year at the Athenaeum. Ten months later, he had finished the supervision of some new construction, the disposal of a stored collection of newspapers, and a complete rearrangement of the library. The Athenaeum was in good condition to be turned over to a successor, and Poole renewed his request to be relieved. By the appointment of Charles Ammi Cutter of the Harvard library, the trustees made it possible for Poole to leave at the end of the year. In its annual report, the Library Committee recited the fact that Poole's resignation had been

received early in the year; but he was requested by the Trustees to remain, till his successor was appointed, which afforded him the opportunity and the Athenaeum the advantage, of bringing his work to a careful and deliberate close. Mr. Poole retires with the best wishes of the Committee for his happiness and prosperity; and the Trustees, at their recommendation, have requested him to continue to avail himself of all the privileges of the Institution.[15]

Presumably as an additional token of approbation, the trustees paid him a "gratuity" of $250.

For almost thirteen years, Poole had served as librarian of the Boston Athenaeum. When he took office, the institution possessed some 60,000 volumes; when he left, it had about 80,000. Its staff had increased significantly. In 1856 the library itself had occupied only the second floor, except for a few collections in virtual storage elsewhere; in 1868 it took up most of the first and second floors and a good part of the third, all of it connected by interior staircases constructed during Poole's term of office and on the basis of his recommendations. The collection during the years had been enriched, most notably by substantial accessions of Civil War newspapers, documents, books, and pamphlets. The acquisition of these materials had been an important accomplishment of his regime, but Poole's major service to the Athenaeum was to preside over its development from only a larger version of a gentleman's library to an operating institutional collection with the specialized staff and the physical arrangements appropriate to such an organization.

Despite the fact that the power and exercise of administrative decision had been retained in large measure by the trustees and their committees, he had been able to recommend wisely enough and to administer forcefully enough to help the institution make the transition. For Poole himself, the experience at the Athenaeum had been valuable. He had deepened his knowledge of bibliography and scholarship. Perhaps most important for his future career, he had been initiated into a kind of library organization that required functional specialization and, for its day, a sizable staff. All of this background was an important prelude to his later work with the large public libraries of the Middle West. In his supervisory capacity, Poole had not learned adequately the administrative skill of delegating responsibility without losing control of operations, but, in the training of the staff, he had achieved some remarkable successes.

It is difficult to know exactly how much credit is due Poole for the later prominence of his subordinates at the Athenaeum, but certainly some of them became notably successful librarians. Mary Abbie Bean, who came in 1860 and remained until 1869, was later well known as the librarian of the Brookline Public Library. Caroline Maria Hewins, who was on the staff in 1866 and 1867, went to the Hartford Library Association (later, the Hartford Public Library) where, as librarian, she pioneered in work with children. Harriet Howe Ames, at the Athenaeum from 1867 to 1869, eventually took charge of the Hoyt Library of East Saginaw, Michigan, perhaps at Poole's recommendation. William Isaac Fletcher, the loyal desk attendant from 1861 to 1866, went successively to the Bronson Library of Waterbury, Connecticut, to the Watkinson Library of Hartford, and then to Amherst College, where he made his greatest reputation. And, in 1866, a young orphan boy sponsored by the Proprietor, Samuel Eliot, took the position at the Athenaeum that turned his life toward the path of great distinction as compiler of the monumental *American Bibliography*. Charles Evans remained at the Athenaeum under Poole and Cutter until 1872, when, on Poole's recommendation, he became the librarian of the Indianapolis Public Library.

As mentor of young librarians, as adviser to the trustees and the Library Committee on practical affairs, as active seeker for new acquisitions, as administrator of the library, and in many smaller ways, Poole, during the years from 1856 to 1868, left his mark on the Athenaeum and on the future course of librarianship in the United States. But at the beginning of 1869, he had no library job. Before the end of that year, he was to guide the fortunes of a number of different libraries in the East and Middle West.

IV. Library Expert, 1869 and Later

The years immediately following Poole's resignation from the Athenaeum were among the busiest of his life. Although a few of his activities were not directly concerned with libraries, his main attention was devoted to his profession. Taking office space in Pemberton Square a few blocks from the Athenaeum, he set himself up as a "library agent." [1] Shortly thereafter, he was commissioned to serve as adviser in the formation of the Silas Bronson Library of Waterbury, Connecticut. He was asked to visit Annapolis for consultation on the reorganization of the Naval Academy Library. He went to Cincinnati at the invitation of the public library's Board of Managers to discuss that library's problems. Also in Cincinnati, he advised Henry Probasco of the public library's board on the cataloging of that gentleman's fine private collection. Even though he eventually became officially Cincinnati's librarian, he continued to serve other libraries as a consultant. In Massachusetts, he helped to select books for the Newton Public Library, the Easthampton Public Library, and the Mount Holyoke Seminary (later Mount Holyoke College). Elsewhere, he advised on purchases for the Fairbanks Library of St. Johnsbury, Vermont, the Grosvenor Library of Buffalo, and, in 1872, the Indianapolis Public Library. All in all, during the four years from 1869 to 1873, he played a part in the affairs of ten different libraries around the country.

In the early part of 1869, Poole also accepted other assignments. At the request of the editor of the Boston *Daily Advertiser*, he reported the Lowell Institute lectures, apparently a paid assignment. He was commissioned by the town of Malden, Massachusetts, to examine the historical background of the various claims to ownership of a large nearby lake important as a source of water, and his report appeared under the title "Who Owns Spot Pond?" in the local paper. He wrote the lead article for the April number of *North American Review*. "Cotton Mather and Salem Witchcraft" was the most comprehensive statement he made of his defense of the old Massachusetts divine against the charge of responsibility for the witchcraft persecutions, but it was only one expression of an interest which he maintained throughout his life.

He continued to hope that a new edition of his *Index* could be published. In 1869, there was talk of a plan whereby the large libraries would join to subsidize its publication, but nothing came of it. Late in 1870, Justin Winsor sought the assistance of Senator Charles Sumner in getting the Smithsonian Institution to pay the publication costs. Sumner forwarded Winsor's letter to Joseph Henry, the Smithsonian's secretary, asking for his opinion. Henry, who had defeated Jewett's plan to make the Smithsonian the national library, replied that, much as he hoped that another source of support could be found for Poole's book, the Institution's funds for the next few years were committed to other projects. When Poole saw Henry's letter, he commented sarcastically:

Prof. Henry's reasons are excellent. The second cannot be beaten: "the preparation of a new orbit for the planet Neptune"! The old one is probably worn out. Let the planet be supplied without delay with so proper an appendage. Without a proper orbit it may be butting against our planet, and disturbing generally the order of the solar system. I hope you will have the letter published. The world ought to know what the "most useless" institution in creation is doing and proposing to do.[2]

Winsor was too much aware of the proprieties to involve himself publicly in such a controversy and too wise to make a fruitless renewal of the old quarrel of librarians with the Smithsonian. With that, the *Index* was shelved to await the cooperative action of the American Library Association a few years later. It was probably just as well for Poole that he could not find a publisher at the moment; he had plenty to keep him busy in his work as "library agent."

The year 1869 was an opportune time for Poole to undertake free-lance work. The movement to form new libraries, which had begun to grow about the middle of the century, had been slowed measurably during the War, but, as soon as peace returned, libraries were started in greater numbers than before all around the country. The trustees of the new libraries took their responsibilities very seriously, especially in the instances when the main impetus for the formation came from a sizable bequest. Very few of the institutions had available in their communities any individual with a substantial background in the operation and management of libraries. The members of the boards felt their own inadequacies to handle the unfamiliar problems. Being often lawyers or business-men, they were able to make some judgments of their own in matters of organization and management; in the field of book selection, they felt themselves much less adequate. The president of one such board said that

after a full consultation, not only with the Executive Committee, but also with several other gentlemen of culture, friends of the Association, it was unanimously agreed that to insure the proper expenditure of so large an amount of money as we saw at the successful termination of the bond scheme would be at the disposal of the Library Committee, it would be necessary to engage the services of some professional li-brarian to supervise the purchase of books. Although among the mem-bers of the Library Committee, and the gentlemen who so kindly gave us their assistance and advice, may be numbered some of the most prominent and best informed literary men of this city, they all assured me that they would not undertake without some such assistance, the selection of so large a number of books; that it required not only a thorough knowledge of books, but a professional experience only to be acquired by studying the literary necessities of the public.

With a considerable need for this sort of assistance and with only a few people of appropriate experience free, Poole found his services sought from many quarters, particularly because he was highly recommended. The president of the Buffalo Young Men's Association was told when he visited Boston "that Mr. Wm. F. Poole was the best man, not only in Boston but in the United States, for our purpose. . . . That recently he had adopted as a profession the organizing of libraries." [3]

Whether Poole was the best in the country or not, he was well prepared for this new occupation. He was able to offer to the boards a thorough knowledge of the records, quarters, and services essen-tial to setting up a library. He could protect them from serious mistakes and oversights in planning; he could recommend to them experienced people to serve as catalogers and as administrators of their institutions; he could give them the benefit of his ability to estimate the amounts and kinds of space, shelving, and equipment that would be required for the sort of library enterprise they could afford. His background in three different libraries had equipped him with a sure knowledge of ways to find answers to the problems of library operation without costly trial and error. Particularly in matters of book selection and acquisition, he had information about publications, patron demand, and the book trade that the board members could not know. His skill at estimating book values was, he said, accurate enough that insurance companies, auctioneers, and book dealers in Boston had often sought his help. The board members might worry that, if they ordered any books before selecting all they would buy, they would find that they had exhausted their funds before completing a well-rounded library. Poole asserted that he could avoid this difficulty and that, in the selection of 10,000 volumes, his estimate of their cost had come within a hundred dollars of the final figure. If the boards would rely on his judgment, they could order piecemeal without waiting to assemble a complete list. In that way, the books could arrive steadily in small batches rather than swamping the libraries by being delivered all at once. Poole could tell the board members how many books could be shelved in a given area and, equally, how much space would be required to house a given number of volumes. He could suggest what he deemed the most convenient and efficient arrangement of quarters. Perhaps most important, he could relieve the board members of the anxieties that came from their being saddled with heavy responsibilities without adequate experience to feel any assurance that they knew what to do. His answers might not always be the best or the only ones, but at least they were rooted in practical experience and would serve.

In addition to his knowledge, his very appearance and manner inspired confidence. Well over six feet tall, he made a commanding figure. A full head of hair was complemented by bushy Dundreary whiskers bristling from the sides of his face and lying down even to his collar, but leaving exposed his strong, smooth-shaven chin. He was not shy and bookish in manner but, rather, a bluff, hearty man who could hold his own in discussion or argument. Not frightened of controversy, he rather relished it. He spoke glibly, with rapid phrases. His conversation was lively, "even vivacious, and always impressive." When he spoke, he looked directly at his listeners. Though his voice was only of medium depth, "he could make it boom" when occasion demanded. The impression he gave was of a man who was "candor itself and straightforward." [4] A member of one social library which consulted Poole recalled his own reaction to the visitor:

I can remember very well the new impression that was made upon me at that time—the revelation, as it were, that the librarian was something more than we had been accustomed to consider him. It was just as though in a country town an architect had been called in to take part in the discussion of plans for a new church, and had given to the people for the first time the idea that the village carpenter was not sufficient for all that ought to be done.[5]

To the businessmen who found the world of libraries unfamiliar and a little frightening, it must have been comforting to have at their side a man who could talk hard facts and figures with the best of them and yet speak with equal positiveness about the mysteries of cataloging, the best leathers for binding, or the most important works of literature. Poole was not known for his delicacy and tact; he could be warm, friendly, and kind, but plain talk was his trade-mark. When he made a recommendation, it was delivered in a tone of finality. Here was a man who could give the board members confidence and reassurance. His price was not small, but that too was a mark of self-esteem which would encourage them to trust him.

The first of the library assignments began in February, 1869, when Poole was employed for a year's term at $2,500 to select and buy books and to advise on the organization of the Silas Bronson Library of Waterbury, Connecticut. The first task was to make up lists of books to buy. In this work, Poole used the Athenaeum, going over that library, alcove by alcove, selecting those books which seemed appropriate to the collection in Waterbury. Orders then went out to book dealers.

After a few months, the time had come to prepare the collection and the building. Doubtless on Poole's recommendation, Fletcher from the Athenaeum was employed as librarian. A capable person for cataloging was absolutely essential. Poole urged a correspondent to hire only a cataloger known to be skilled, for

they are in the end the cheapest sort of cataloguers to employ. . . . Employ a blacksmith to build your house; get a cobbler to make you a carriage, but don't put an incompetent to work on a catalogue. A little knowledge in these matters is a dangerous, very dangerous thing. If you can't get a skilled person, get an intelligent, well educated person who knows *nothing* about cataloguing. They are ready to receive instructions.[6]

Fletcher had already received instructions at the Athenaeum. With Poole's advice and direction, he began to prepare the various records and the books themselves. Each volume was entered in an accession book, a shelf list, and a manuscript catalog; it was also given a call number and prepared for the shelves with book plate and ownership stamps. Soon it was time to consider printing the catalog.

Poole thought a printed catalog was essential. He remonstrated vigorously with Justin Winsor of the Boston Public Library when it was proposed to abandon a printed catalog there. Complicated procedures, he said, were not needed; the thing to do was to simplify the methods so as to be able to provide a printed catalog. The public would not be satisfied without one. Winsor would "have a howling about [his] ears which will not be agreeable." No elaborate scheme was required. "The practical want of the public, I believe, is a simple finding catalogue." And the objection that no supplement could be final—that soon another would be required—was no argument at all. "It is the reason of the woman who didn't wash her dishes. Go on, and make the 4th, and the 20th if need be." A catalog was a practical necessity and a legitimate demand of the public.[7]

All of the preliminaries were in line with one of Poole's cardinal principles, that no library should be opened to the public until it had a collection of books appropriate to the community in size and content. Although it was wise not to delay so long as to cause the public's interest to decline, nothing could be more foolish than to lend the books before they had been properly recorded or to open with such a small collection that the patrons would find the new library a disappointment.

Accordingly, the Bronson Library was not opened until fourteen months after Poole's appointment. In the new library, the pattern of service reflected the benevolent but paternalistic aims of the public libraries of the time. Here was to be a collection of books open, not just to the genteel members of a private society, but to all of the public, including the workers in the local mills. Of the rules adopted during Poole's first year in Cincinnati, one of the first said, "Ample arrangements having been made for washing, the attendants are instructed to deliver no periodical or book into unclean hands." [8] With such a view of the expected users, it was natural that the books should be kept on closed shelves, as in the Brothers Library or the Mercantile Library, rather than on open shelves, as in the Athenaeum. A delivery desk separated the readers from the books. Loans were recorded in a ledger or "register," with one page allotted to each borrower. With closed shelves, a catalog for public use was a prime necessity; one in printed form was ready two months after the library opened. In line with the common arrangement of the times, there was, in addition to the library itself, a sizable reading room for periodicals and newspapers. The library, its collections, and its organization were found to be highly satisfactory to the board, the librarian, and the public, a result for which Poole was given generous credit.

In the essentials, Poole had supervised in Waterbury the whole process of getting a library on its feet. In other instances, his duties were more restricted. In Newton, he received $300 for the preparation of a buying list and some general advice. Fletcher, though remaining in Waterbury, was employed to prepare the copy for the catalog and to supervise its printing. The experience in Newton and in Waterbury was valuable preparation for the day when the team of Poole and Fletcher would make the third edition of the *Index*. For the Naval Academy, Poole devised a broad classification, advised on cataloging procedures, and put the officials in touch with two capable catalogers who had been trained in the Athenaeum. He also worked in limited ways with the St. Johnsbury, Easthampton, and Mount Holyoke libraries.

In 1872 Poole undertook for a fee of $300 to select some 8,000 volumes for the Indianapolis Public Library and to advise on other matters. As in Waterbury, one of his protégés, in this case

Charles Evans, was brought in to become librarian and to make the catalog. Poole himself, after a period as adviser to the Cincinnati Public Library, became its librarian. His preoccupation with the affairs of that library was one factor in his difficulties with another of his assignments.

For a fee of $1,500, Poole was employed to serve for a year as adviser to the Grosvenor Library of Buffalo. The main part of his assignment was to be the preparation of lists of books for purchase, but he was to advise on the other aspects of library operation as well, working with the librarian, Alexander J. Sheldon. Difficulties arose because the trustees feared that, if they bought books before they had the complete list in hand, they would spend all of their money before they had assembled a well-balanced collection. Poole assured them that it was his professional duty to prevent that result and, furthermore, that it would be a mistake to wait to order, thus swamping Sheldon with all the books at one time. It would be quite safe to order the books on individual subjects as Poole finished each subject list, a task that went along reasonably well, although delayed at times by his attention to other libraries. With his usual self-confidence, Poole thought the trustees accepted his arguments. They, on the other hand, stood on their conviction that, as employers, they were under no necessity to heed his arguments or even to indicate their lack of agreement. The result was that Poole went his way, preparing lists, and the trustees went theirs, filing the lists when received but not ordering the books. By the time it became apparent that the two parties did not understand each other, too much rancor had been generated to allow further discussion or any final agreement. After many months, during which Poole was never paid, he discovered that the Grosvenor trustees were using other agents to serve them. Interpreting this action as bad faith, he quietly abandoned any further work. When Poole applied some time later to a succeeding board of trustees for payment of fees to cover at least his out-of-pocket expenses, the original trustees simply denounced him. Eventually Poole was paid a compromise amount, and with that the incident closed.

Neither side handled the matter with entire credit. The trouble was a failure on both sides to keep the other fully informed and to thrash out the differences to a clear conclusion. Each depended upon a kind of righteous assignment of fault to the other, and neither insisted upon arguing out the problems. Poole accepted too easily the fact—unquestionably true—that library boards in the nineteenth century had absolute authority. Not only did they have the power but they had no guidelines as to the proper methods and limits of its exercise. Years had to pass, librarians had to resign or be fired, libraries had to fall into decay and confusion for lack of effective executive action, and administrative theory had to be developed, before librarian-board relationships could be improved. In fact, of course, many librarians of the time were able to command enough respect from their boards to be allowed to exercise the authority that theoretically remained in board hands. Poole himself clearly did so at the Brothers Library, at the Mercantile Library, at Waterbury, and at Cincinnati. His confidence that the board at the Grosvenor would come around to his view of the proper timing of book orders led him to delay too long in trying to persuade them directly. Although his place as a consultant rather than as librarian made the issue somewhat less than clear-cut, he had been employed—so he thought—for professional services which went beyond mere advice. His failure to understand the issues clearly and to state them plainly did not help to develop the background for good organizational theory. Had he acted differently, the Grosvenor episode might have stood in the history of library administration as an important test case along with Winsor's dramatic resignation from the Boston Public Library in 1877. But Poole had no time for controversy; he was busy in Cincinnati.

V. Cincinnati Public Library, 1869-1873

The Cincinnati Public Library was started in 1853 with a group of books distributed under the Ohio law of that year which provided for libraries as a part of the equipment of the schools. The proceeds of a special tax were used to buy books for distribution to boards of education throughout the state. Although distribution was based on the pupil population, all of the people had access to the libraries. The library tax, being especially unpopular with the smaller towns and villages, was first suspended and then, in 1860, repealed.

During the next seven years the Cincinnati Public Library struggled to maintain itself while its collection dwindled. Salaries and other expenses, which were met from the Cincinnati Board of Education's general funds, continued to be paid, but the only support for the book collection came from fines and donations. Finally, in 1867, the library advocates managed, by limiting the law's application to large communities, to secure authorization for the boards of education to levy a tax on those cities only. At about the same time, the legislature authorized appointment of a separate board of managers for the library. The new board, however, was appointed by the Board of Education and subservient to it. This subordination of the library was characterized by one library governing board as a

most ingeniously contrived blunder, by which the managers have to plan and prepare all the measures necessary for the Institution without the power of executing them, and the Board of Education have to execute all those measures without the means of knowing anything about them.[1]

This arrangement produced some notable abuses and some spectacular battles as various factions in the remote Board of Education sought to displace the librarian with their own candidates.

Despite certain defects, the legal changes of 1867 helped the library. It was, however, still in poor condition in 1869. Housed in inadequate quarters in the Ohio Mechanics' Institute, it was crowded and dirty. Its three-man staff could barely maintain the eleven-hour daily schedule of service and had time to keep up, as a record of the collection, only an accession book. There was hope for the future, however. The Board of Education bought centrally located property and began construction of a building. The library's board determined to obtain expert assistance. Poole was recommended, and, without consulting him, the board elected him its librarian at a salary of $2,500. This election was a formality made necessary by the fact that the board could pay a salary only to a man on the regular payroll. When Poole visited Cincinnati, he explained that he had other commitments, but he offered to accept a term appointment with the provision that he would spend at least half of his time in the city.

Poole's acceptance of the appointment in Cincinnati did not at all mean that he had decided to make his home in the Middle West. He was frequently back in Melrose with his family, and he never moved them to Cincinnati. Even so, by 1872 he had become enthusiastic about the opportunities in the region. He wrote to Evans: "The West is a big country, and I advise you to come out here. . . . There are opportunities out here for a person to get all he can earn." [2]

Cincinnati was a prime example of the opportunities to be found in the Middle West. A prosperous city of about 200,000, it had both wealth and the cultural interests characteristic of a predominantly German population. Its literary club, the oldest in the country, had been founded in 1849. So young was the public library movement that Cincinnati's library was already a leading pioneer in the nation. No other library could rival the great Boston Public Library under Justin Winsor's administration, but Cincinnati nosed out both New Bedford and Worcester, Massachusetts, for second place. Its newly assured annual income of $13,000 for books and its prospective new building would soon enable it to outdistance either of them. Clearly, the Cincinnati Public Library had a bright future, though much work had to be done.

Poole's first recommendation was that a catalog should be prepared. He arranged that the work should be done in Boston, where he could employ skilled catalogers who would have access to the Athenaeum's bibliographical collection. Working from the accession book, they finished a 40,000-card catalog by the end of May, 1870, and in 1871 the catalog was printed in book form.

In Cincinnati, book purchases were limited to current publications in order not to strain the already crowded quarters. When, in June, 1870, the building was not completed as had been hoped, Poole's appointment was extended to October 1. Beginning in September, the library was closed for a period of twelve weeks while the furniture and book collection were installed. Poole's appointment was again extended, this time to the end of 1870.

Finally, on December 8, 1870, the new building was dedicated. It included reading rooms containing periodicals and reference books on the first floor and book stacks and a delivery desk on the second. Although patrons could call for books to be delivered for reading downstairs, they had to go to the second floor to borrow for home use. One advantage of the direct contact between reader and attendant which seemed important to Poole was that, if the desired book was not in, the patron could have the benefit of the attendant's help in selecting a suitable substitute.

At first, the library recorded loans in the customary ledger book, with one page for each borrower. Later, under pressure of greatly expanded use, Poole adopted a system devised by Fletcher for the Bronson Library. Loans were recorded on slips, which were filed by date of issue. The new system was quicker than the old, especially because service to men and women was separated, dividing the work load.

During the first three months in new quarters, the number of registered borrowers rose from 7,400 to more than 10,000. Circulation, which had been about 1,000 volumes per week before the move, jumped dramatically, finally stabilizing between three and four times the old rate. During the days of this boom, Poole remained to superintend the library, for, on January 23, 1871, he had accepted a full-time appointment at a salary of $3,000, effective December 9, the first day of operation in the new building.

In all respects, the new library was prospering. Here was a brand new building with 200 seats, 300 current periodicals, and a book collection which grew during the first three months from 22,000 to 28,000 volumes. On March 12, 1871, the library took a bold new step to increase its usefulness by opening the reading rooms on Sunday. Cincinnati thus became the first large municipal library to make its facilities available on the Sabbath. In making this change, Cincinnati reaped the benefit of having a liberal community in contrast to the Puritan conservatives who had blocked such a move in Boston. Although the new hours of opening did not immediately prove their worth, Poole recommended a full year's trial, and the experiment was successful. He was also proud that he was able to take the annual inventory without closing the library. In the future, the library was to be open every day of the year.

In order to meet the expanded demands for service, the staff was increased to eight full-time and eight part-time employees, in addition to the janitor. The book collection grew not just by purchase but also by the deposit of the collections of other organizations. In buying books, one principal aim had been to strengthen the collection of popular fiction. Although Poole would exclude immoral or vicious books and not attempt entirely to meet a transitory first demand, he was vigorous in maintaining that

prose fiction, judiciously selected, meets the legitimate and healthful wants of the community, and . . . no public library, supported by the taxes of the whole people, could maintain public sympathy and support if it did not supply the books which the people wish to read.

While he recognized their "feebleness and insipidity," the novels of authors like Mrs. Southworth "meet the wants of a crude and uncultivated literary taste, which could not appreciate Jane Eyre or Romola; and perhaps they help to educate it for something better." Even if no improvement of taste, in fact, did occur, such volumes "perform a beneficent mission, as they are read by females in the intervals of their daily toil in the workshop and the family, and thus relieve the tedium of a hard lot." [3] This purpose, if accepted, made the case for novels in the library impregnable. The board was cautious in accepting Poole's position, objecting mainly on moral grounds, but also concerned that the loan of fiction was steadily requiring the addition of new employees. Within a year five more full-time assistants joined the eight previously employed.

Books more substantial than popular fiction were also bought, including works of French and German literature, which were imported, and second-hand books, which were bought at auction. Most European books were obtained from the dealer whom Poole regularly used, B. F. Stevens of London. After considerable investigation, Poole settled on G. Deuerlich of Göettingen to supply the German books so much in demand in Cincinnati. In the auction market, Poole showed that he had learned a good deal during his experience at the Athenaeum. When his agent complained that the limits on price were sometimes too low, Poole replied that "these random shots do sometimes take the game." On another occasion, when he wanted to buy a set from which two particular volumes were commonly missing, he suggested, even though he wanted the incomplete set, that the agent "question the fact at the sale and frighten the buyers." Again, a certain work was sent at Cincinnati's limit price despite the fact that ostensibly it had been sold at the auction at a higher price. He wrote: "I don't like the principle of having lots tooted up by the auctioneer or the owners, and then falling back on the highest limit that is given by a genuine bidder. I can't have that played on me." Back the volumes went to the auction house. As it happened, principle and self-interest coincided, since the set was found, on examination, to be rather a poor copy. [4]

Obtaining foreign books posed two main problems. The long delays in the transport of shipments to Cincinnati and in the sending of money to Europe made the dealers unwilling to wait to receive payment. Equally, however, the library was reluctant to tie up large sums of money on deposit in European banks. Poole arranged with a sewing-machine manufacturer to honor drafts of book dealers in Europe and to submit the bills to the library for payment. Everyone benefited: the dealers in prompt payment, the library in free use of its funds, and the manufacturer in not having to transfer substantial sums of cash across the Atlantic. The second problem involved the technicalities required by the United States Customs Office in admitting books for the library duty-free. By extensive and patient correspondence, Poole arranged that his shipments were properly marked and handled and finally was able to establish a procedure whereby the shipments were sent in bond to Cincinnati, where they could be inspected more quickly than on the East Coast. All of these details and expedients required the kind of sure hand which Poole's long experience had given him.

Some of the books thus acquired were destined for a special department. In recognition of the library's possession of many large illustrated works and of the interest in art in the city, Poole recommended that one of the third-floor rooms be set up as a departmental library for art, perhaps the first subject department in an American public library. There the books could have the special protection they required, and the patrons could have the benefit of unusual equipment, such as large tables and easels. Such a room would attract not only art students but also engineers and designers from the local manufacturing plants—an eminently practical use, Poole pointed out, since good taste in design of manufactured articles added to their sales value. Poole thus was seeking the support of the practical businessman with a special service, just as he sought that of the general public by furnishing novels.

In addition to serving the general readers, the art students, and the businessmen, Poole gave attention to the children by expanding the collection of juvenile books in recognition of the fact that those sixteen and younger constituted 22 percent of the registrants. This was only one more example of his effort to serve the whole community.

Everything ran smoothly, but there were some problems. Some books were stolen, in one notable case a substantial number of theological books, which were found in the room of a young ministerial student. The leniency shown the offender displeased Poole, who consistently advocated unremitting pursuit of violators and firm punishment of those apprehended. Only in this way, he

said, could the collection be protected without unwarranted restrictions on services to honest patrons. Winsor agreed:

We do not measure the extent of an endeavor to recover books by the
value of the particular one lost. . . . [Boston's] immunity from loss
comes from a rigid system of following up delinquents, which we have
been practising for twenty-five years, for our gain and for the moral
advantage of our citizens. . . . The result of that discipline has been
that we have found we could trust the public more and more.[5]

Perhaps because public libraries were new enough that all were
conscious that library books were municipal property, the librarians were able to obtain considerable cooperation from the
police in enforcing a strict policy.

The problem of crowding in the new quarters was only temporary, for, in accordance with plans made from the beginning,
two additional structures were rising behind the building already
occupied. A two-story structure would connect the existing building with a great hall at the rear of the lot. The occupation of the
whole building would inaugurate a new day for the Cincinnati
Public Library. The great hall—the main reading room—would
provide ample space for readers. Around its perimeter, five levels
of book stacks would rise almost to the ceiling. On the second
floor of the front building, the room for borrowers would be on
the same level as the most-used books in the great hall, with the
circulation desk between them. This arrangement would minimize
the disadvantage of having books on five different levels, since the
books most in demand would be housed and loaned on the same
floor level. Whether because he knew that the plans were too far
advanced to be changed when he arrived or whether he had not
yet developed his strong opposition to galleries, Poole did not
criticize the plans of his library, although it was a good example
of the kind of building he attacked unmercifully in later years.
He told Winsor that it was not the best building which could be
planned but that it would be the best in the country. Some people
in Cincinnati felt that a building with a capacity for 250,000 volumes was too large for a collection which initially numbered a
tenth of that size. Poole pointed out that accessions of only 15,000
per year would more than occupy all the space in twenty years
and commented that "the life of the library is not twenty years,

nor fifty years; but, let us hope, for all time." [6] Even in the brief
time Poole was librarian, 40,000 volumes were acquired, making
his 1871 catalog out of date. He suggested that the occupancy
of the whole building would be an opportune time to print a
supplement, a task which would be made easy by the fact that
the new accessions were already recorded in an up-to-date card
catalog. In all respects, nothing but the brightest future was in
sight.

Despite all of his work in Cincinnati and elsewhere, Poole had
not abandoned his historical studies. He found time in 1870
to examine the original, mud-tracked manuscript of Governor
Thomas Hutchinson's *History of Massachusetts* in the state archives at Boston, and, discovering there an earlier and fuller text
than had been printed, he published the section dealing with
Salem witchcraft, accompanied by his own extensive notes. Also
during that year, he wrote two brief responses to a critical reply
to his Mather article by Charles W. Upham, the originator—so
Poole maintained—of the anti-Mather theory. Some years before
he left the Athenaeum, he had received formal permission from
their library committee to copy a pamphlet from Washington's
library, *Anti-Slavery Opinions before the Year 1800,* by Dr. George
Buchanan. In a long introduction to the reprint, Poole maintained
that, during those early years, such anti-slavery opinions had not
been divided on a sectional basis.

Another volume Poole published in 1870 was a description of
the Tyler Davidson Fountain recently erected in the center of
the city by Henry Probasco, book collector and former library
board member, in honor of his brother-in-law. Although the work
of the library in 1871 seems to have been enough to take up Poole's
time in that year, he was very active outside the library in 1872.
In November, he read a paper on his anti-slavery topic before
the Cincinnati Literary Club, of which he was a devoted member. And, in December, he read another on the connection of
Dr. Manasseh Cutler with the Ordinance of 1787. Based on the
venerable minister's journal, which was still preserved by the
family in Marietta, Ohio, Poole's study maintained that Cutler
had been the catalyst who made possible the Ordinance's remarkable provisions for the support of public education and the ban-

ning of slavery in the Northwest Territory. The "Poole theory" of the origins of the Ordinance was elaborated in great detail in his article, which finally appeared in the *North American Review* in 1876. As written there, it was one of his most sophisticated historical studies, particularly in its identification of the economic motives behind the ostensibly altruistic provisions of the Ordinance. Poole maintained that Cutler, taking advantage of the Southern wish to sell public lands to pay off the national debt, had won acceptance of the humanitarian provisions as a way of appealing to prospective New England purchasers.

This historical study and the participation in literary discussions with leading business and political figures doubtless helped Poole make a place for himself and for the library on the local scene. Some of the evident support which he obtained as librarian came from friendships he made through these channels. This kind of personal following was particularly important in the situation produced by the strange division of authority between the Board of Education and the library's board of managers. Poole was never seriously threatened by the factionalism which, in later times, produced political battles between the supporters of rival candidates for the librarianship. The board of managers rewarded Poole with consistent support, an increase in salary to $3,500 in the middle of 1872, and generous praise. Speaking of the progress, they gave

credit for much the larger share to the Librarian . . . who, not only by the thorough professional skill and acquirements which he has brought to our aid, but by his devotion and unremitting industry in the work of organizing and building up the Library, has justly entitled himself to this special mark of our thanks.[7]

Despite the strong position which the board's support gave him in Cincinnati, Poole could not resist another great opportunity when it presented itself. Late in 1873 he decided to accept an offer to become librarian of the Chicago Public Library, which was just being formed.

When the news of Poole's resignation became public, a number of candidates sought the position. There was a good deal of talk about trying to retain Poole by raising his salary to $5,000. That proposal was opposed by a coalition representing many factions. The *Catholic Telegraph* objected to the very existence of the public library, which it considered an outlaw institution, illegally supported by taxation. The previous summer, the local archbishop had raised a mild storm by forbidding Catholic children to visit the repository of what he considered immoral books, nor was he mollified when Poole, on examining the book in question, agreed that it was not proper and withdrew it from circulation. The German newspapers conceded that Poole was "ein sehr guter Bibliothekar," [8] but they opposed any salary increase. The Cincinnati *Commercial*, whose assistant editor, Thomas Vickers, was a candidate for the librarianship, joined the weekly Cincinnati *Post* in attacking Poole's administration. They charged that the catalog could have been prepared by any clerk, that a certain book purchase had been unwise, and that there might be something corrupt about the arrangement with the sewing-machine manufacturer to pay bills abroad. The *Daily Gazette* and the *Daily Enquirer* supported the raise in pay. Most of the opposition was stated on grounds of the extravagant amount proposed rather than personal opposition to Poole. Poole said, after the opposition developed, that his previous resignation had been based on a firm commitment to Chicago and that he was not free to accept any offer that Cincinnati might make. He did not hesitate to express his views as to suitable appointees. Although his recommendations apparently were made privately, his opinions must have become public knowledge. Vickers was decidedly not one of those whom Poole recommended, but he was the man elected. The two men sniped at each other during the next several years, Poole in letters to his Cincinnati friends and Vickers in published form. But even Vickers's violently partisan journalistic supporter was unable to sustain any serious charge against Poole's administration.

After Vickers's appointment, a difficulty with one of the contractors delayed completion of the building and made it clear that the dedication would be later than expected. Characteristically, Poole was more interested in getting on with his new work than with tidying up the old. When Charles Evans had suggested spending two weeks at the Athenaeum to put his work in order before going to Indianapolis, Poole replied: "What do you care about fixing up things? Let them attend to that. You are wanted here. Kiss the young lady you are courting, and leave town." [9]

Taking his own advice in at least its last particular, Poole arranged to conclude his own service on January 1, 1874.

In leaving Cincinnati, Poole was turning over to Vickers a thriving institution which soon would occupy its great new hall. He left behind a collection of more than 60,000 volumes, two thirds of it acquired during his four years there. Most of the staff had been trained by him. The books had been classified and cataloged, the building constructed, the procedures established, a portion of the quarters arranged, and plans made for the remaining changes. The people of Cincinnati had been introduced under his administration to the services of a large and active public library. Although, after Poole left, Vickers criticized and changed many features of Poole's administration, he did not succeed in discrediting Poole or his work. When, twenty-five years afterward, a later president of the library's board came to write a history of the institution, he could still say of Poole's original appointment: "The selection of that master librarian was the best stroke of library policy ever made by the board of managers of the Public Library." [10] All in all, Poole's Cincinnati stay was the most satisfactory single period of his career. He had been fortunate enough to come on the scene at a time when the city's library affairs were at a flood. He had been provided with generous funds and full support and had known how to take advantage of both. The results were highly satisfactory to himself, to his board, and to the citizens of the community. It might have been more difficult to leave behind had not the future promised even more.

VI. Chicago Public Library, 1874-1879

The promise for the future of the Chicago Public Library was exceeded only by the expectations for the city itself. Hardly two years before Poole's arrival, in October, 1871, the community had been devastated by one of the most spectacular and destructive fires in the history of the country. To the wonder of the whole world, the city had picked itself up and shrugged off its disaster as a mere incident in its progress toward what it confidently thought was its destiny to become the greatest city in the nation. With a population of over 300,000, a location athwart the transportation lines of the country, large processing, manufacturing, and commercial establishments, and a rich hinterland pouring in wealth, Chicago had a brilliant future which clearly included the economic resources to support a public library. Although still a wild and brawling community, it had already developed the leaders who could give direction to new ventures. Not content merely with rebuilding its business and industrial life after the Fire, they had laid the foundations for a new cultural institution as well. On January 1, 1873, the new Chicago Public Library had opened the doors of its reading room.

Even before the Fire, community leaders had been taking steps toward the establishment of a free public library. Poole himself had visited the city only a few weeks before the Fire and had talked with Editor Horace White of the Chicago *Tribune*, who had been advocating the idea. Although the recovery of the city from devastation occupied everyone's attention for a brief time, the interested leaders soon returned to their work of creating a library. In this venture, they were spurred on by the efforts of a denominational library to seize leadership and by the news that a group in England was engaged in collecting books to send as a gift to the city. It was essential, if only as a matter of civic pride, that a suitable, secular institution be prepared to receive the gift. As Gwladys Spencer has shown in all detail, the Chicago Public Library was born because the fundamental preconditions for such an institution existed; the impetus of the Fire and its aftermath was only the precipitating factor.[1] Valid as is the thesis of multiple causation in this connection, the importance of the Fire should not be discounted. The disaster and the events which led from it were clearly decisive in regard to the timing of the establishment and the form that it took. Had the Fire not occurred, the course of library history in Chicago would have been quite different. The development would have been evolutionary, would have been based on foundations already laid by one or more of the city's social libraries, and would have been delayed in its accomplishment. The point is important because financial difficulties during the early years of the library give some reason to suppose that the new institution came into being before the community was entirely ready for it.

Whether the city was ready or not, its leaders moved quickly. After two mass meetings, they sent a delegation to Springfield to urge early passage of a library law already being considered. Sponsored by Erastus Swift Willcox of Peoria, who had solicited advice from Poole and Winsor in the drafting, the bill was amended to meet the special needs of Chicago and was speedily passed as an emergency measure. On April 1, 1872, the city council adopted an ordinance establishing the Chicago Public Library, and the Mayor proceeded to name the board of directors. In July, the first employee, William Bailey Wickersham, was appointed as secretary and then, in December, also as acting librarian. By that time arrangements had been made to house the library in the famous "Book Tank." This structure was one of the strangest ever to shelter a public library. Originally designed as a water reservoir, it consisted of an iron tank resting thirty feet high on a stone foundation. To adapt it for library use, a brick wall was built around the inside, walnut flooring was laid over the iron deck, and shelves were constructed around the walls. A stairway led down from the Tank to the roof of a two-story building which had been hastily thrown up after the Fire to house the municipal offices. There on the top of this structure, known as the Rookery, a partial third story had been built to provide a reading room and office space for the library.

By June of 1873, the library had almost 7,000 volumes in the Tank. While visitors were welcome to see the new library, only the periodicals and books in the reading room could be consulted, and none could be borrowed. The rooms were open from nine to nine daily, including Sundays, and had about three hundred visitors each day.

All of these preparations were preliminary. The board was well aware that the quarters then occupied would not be suitable for long. Negotiations were under way to exchange some land belonging to the Board of Education for the site of the ruins of the post office. Just as the Tank was unsuitable as permanent quarters, so the directors thought they needed as librarian a man more thoroughly experienced in library operation than Wickersham. Winsor was invited to accept the position, but he declined to leave Boston. Then, on October 25, 1873, the board held a special meeting, for which Poole had been invited to Chicago, and authorized his appointment. The $4,000 salary and the challenge of an unformed library were sufficient to entice Poole away even from the attractions of occupying a great new building in Cincinnati.

The generous salary provision was an indication of the earnestness of the directors' desire to get the best man available. And there can be no doubt that, taking length of experience as the gauge, Poole was that man. No one in the nation could compare with him except the Bostonian who was rooted to his own locale. Not even Winsor could present in his credentials such an extended and varied background as Poole, whose library career went back more than twenty-five years and encompassed the oldest mercantile library, the foremost social library, and the second largest public library in the country.

The board's action in finding a leading librarian and paying him well was in line with the optimistic expectations for a new library in Chicago. When, on the morning of January 2, 1874, Poole stepped down from the train and made his way to Matteson House, where he was to live for almost six months, he could look

forward to assuming the responsibility for a library which he and
its directors confidently expected would soon be foremost in the
nation. On that day, Poole began an administration which was
to last more than thirteen years. With Winsor's move to Harvard
in 1877, Poole's position as first public librarian of the land was
beyond dispute. In thirteen years, the Chicago Public Library
would grow to possess 129,000 volumes, to have 29,000 borrowers registered on its rolls, to circulate more than 625,000 volumes
annually, and to spend more than $70,000 each year. These ac-
complishments would be attended with many difficulties and, in
sum, were less than Poole had reason to foresee when he started
out in 1874.

Some of the difficulties could hardly have been expected; the
Illinois law of 1872 had been carefully drafted to avoid them.
Though the directors were to be named by the mayor and confirmed by the city council, they were to be free from interference
by that body, not more than one of whose members could serve
on the library's board at any given time. All money received for
library purposes was to be placed in a special fund which, though
deposited in the city treasury, was to be drawn upon only by
vouchers of the board. The Illinois plan on its face was designed
to avoid the control by an outside body which plagued public libraries in Ohio and Indiana. No doubt the Cincinnati difficulties
in this respect were among the problems which Poole warned
against when Willcox sought advice on a draft of the Illinois
library law.

Some time later, Poole had occasion to give advice on library
problems in a more comprehensive and public way. Written for
the guidance of those in charge of new libraries, his statement
amounted to a distillation of the conclusions which he had reached
up to that time about many aspects of the theory and practice of
librarianship. It served the twin functions of describing in some
detail how he had gone about the task of setting up public library
service in Chicago and of expressing his views on library principles and practices. His definition of a public library, which has
been used down to recent times as a classic, clearly specified the
need for legislation to authorize a municipality to set up a library
and to use tax money to support it:

The "public library" which we are to consider is established by state laws, is supported by local taxation and voluntary gifts, is managed as a public trust, and every citizen of the city or town which maintains it has an equal share in its privileges of reference and circulation.

In regard to the Ohio and Indiana plans, he said, in echo of the words of Cincinnati's board in 1871:

The obvious objection to this system is that the real control of the library is with a board of many members who were appointed for other duties, and have not the time or inclination to make themselves familiar with the details of library management. They are required to vote upon subjects on which they have little or no practical knowledge.

The Illinois law took care of this problem, but it failed in other respects to achieve the kind of independence for the board which its provisions seemed to specify. The board was, nevertheless, a separate agency of the city government with broad powers to control library affairs. In turn, the library's by-laws gave the librarian substantial executive power.[2]

When Poole took office, he was under injunction from the directors to proceed as quickly as possible to provide for the circulation of books. The library had been in existence for almost two years, and its reading room had been open for a full twelve months. Sentiment in the city was beginning to be impatient for books to be lent for home use. This goal had been prominent among the board's purposes for some time. The directors had recognized early that, valuable though the donations were, the character of the gifts tended toward substantial works which were more suitable for reference and study than for general circulation. They were convinced that one of the library's important functions should be the provision of books for popular reading. So anxious were they to prepare for lending that they had bought books especially adapted to that purpose even before Poole came as librarian and at a time when they were not adding substantially to the collection by purchase. During the year ending June, 1873, the library bought only 978 volumes. Of these, 786 were works of British authors in the Tauchnitz edition, which was thought to be especially suitable for a circulating library. The purchase may have been made at Poole's recommendation, for he was acting as agent for Baron Tauchnitz and supplied sets to a number of libraries, of which Chicago may well have been one.

Before the library could be opened, there was much to be done. The first steps had already been taken to fill the need for adequate quarters. In none of the essentials were the Book Tank and the adjoining Rookery reading room suitable for an active public library of the kind envisioned for Chicago. In fact, Poole had recommended in October that the bizarre structure be abandoned.

The directors had concluded, from the protracted nature of the negotiations, that the site of the old post office would not be available in the near future. Accordingly, they had decided to rent quarters. A number of new commercial structures were available in the business center of the city, and, even before Poole arrived, the board had rented all of the second and half of the third and fourth floors in a building at the corner of Wabash and Madison. The day after taking office, Poole presented to the board plans for arrangement of the space. The necessary alterations and equipment were put under contract almost immediately.

Poole thought the board's action very wise. "This is not the time to talk of building permanent quarters." [3] In his advice to new library boards, he warned that few could command the funds and experience to build at the start a structure which would be satisfactory for long. Libraries, he said, grow very quickly and, as they grow, their requirements change. "A library of 100,000 volumes needs not only a larger building than one of 20,000 volumes, but a different kind of building." [4] At the outset, however, the essentials were few; sufficient, well-lighted space easily reached in a building located in the center of the community would meet the requirements. Quarters on the ground floor were preferable, but an upper story would be satisfactory; not only would the rent be cheaper, but the light might well be better. Chicago's new building fit the case exactly.

With the work on the quarters under way, it was time to acquire the books needed for a large circulating library. After only a month Poole presented for the board's approval a list of 27,000 volumes, including 10,000 American, 12,000 English, 3,500 German, and 1,500 French and Italian publications. In making his selections, he must surely have had in mind the principles which he commended to library organizers. The board should remember that the function of a public library was to supply books for all groups in the community. The persons making the selection, therefore, should not depend exclusively on their own tastes but should remember that, poor as some of the books might be, they would help to cultivate the habit of reading and make available works with which inexperienced readers could begin their climb to better taste. Equally, books for the young and for educated readers should be provided. All in all, if the board took into account the interests of all the various groups in the community, the selection was likely to be satisfactory. In doing this work himself during his activity as "library agent," Poole had used the collection of the Athenaeum as a source of titles to consider. Since the directors of other libraries would not be so fortunate as to have that resource available, he suggested that the printed catalogs of the larger libraries would be helpful.

Poole was not severely hampered in his purchases by a lack of funds. The library's tax income had been substantial and was expected to increase. Other libraries—such as those in Waterbury and Buffalo—had generous endowments. For libraries without substantial founding funds, Poole suggested several alternatives. They might form their initial book collections by allowing tax money to accumulate for a time, by soliciting gifts of money and books from local citizens, and by persuading local social libraries to donate their books.

Even having made a beginning, most libraries would not be able to buy all the books they wanted. For such a situation, Poole recommended that a board buy first the popular works which would be sought by patrons at the start, leaving technical books and those of a scholarly nature until later. But at least a basic reference collection, including encyclopedias, dictionaries, and gazetteers, should be a part of any library from the beginning. As a start in assembling the desired popular works, Poole suggested a number of sets, including the Tauchnitz edition, which he gave a special commendation, though without going so far as to name himself as the agent. Even for Chicago with its generous funds, Poole concentrated primarily on buying popular titles.

With more than 7,000 volumes, mostly substantial works of permanent value received as gifts before he arrived, he could afford to emphasize popular works. Convinced that the Tauchnitz collection provided excellent books at low cost, he recommended more than 5,000 duplicates from that series as well as extra copies of other popular works, with the intention of providing enough copies to meet the demand for books of established merit.

Although fortunate at the outset in being able to duplicate freely in Chicago, Poole advised libraries forced to decide between extensive duplication and wide coverage to choose the latter. When, shortly afterward, the Chicago financial pinch began, he followed this principle by a drastic reduction in the number of copies of popular titles he bought. Where duplication was possible, he recommended, as a standard of judgment, that as many copies be bought as would meet "the permanent demand for a book of real merit" but not "the first and temporary demand for a new book." [5]

In selecting serials, Poole recommended that every library should have important periodicals and that the larger ones should make available copies of the leading newspapers, as he did in Chicago. He thought that boards of smaller libraries might very properly decide to use their limited income for more valuable publications than newspapers. Strangely, he did not suggest to the boards the expedient—used by him in Boston, Cincinnati, and Chicago —of obtaining many of the newspapers as gifts of the publishers.

Finally, as regards selection, Poole advised library directors on the matter about which he had been unable to convince the directors of the Grosvenor. A library board could know in advance approximately how many books a given amount of money would buy even without detailed lists of titles and prices. A good circulating library collection could be bought for an average price of $1.25 per volume. Such an average would allow the acquisition of some titles running ten times as much per volume and would cover the cost of the necessary reference books.

Poole's reputation as a shrewd book buyer was earned over many years, during which he learned a number of different techniques. For foreign books he recommended buying through an agent overseas in order to obtain the advantages of a cheaper price and a binding (which in that case could be done abroad) that was better and less expensive than if done in the United States. Libraries—as he had occasion to know from the war years of high tariffs at the Athenaeum—had an advantage in importing their own books, which, under those circumstances, were free of duty. The agent selected would buy the desired titles and would invoice them to the library at the cost price, adding a reasonable commission. Current American books should be bought by competitive bid, not for individual titles but for the rate of discount, a figure which would usually range from 25 to 35 percent. In 1874, the successful bid in Chicago was 35 percent, as low a price, Poole claimed, as ever commanded by a library.

Most of the books bought in Chicago at first were in-print titles readily acquired. When the time came to buy other sorts of books, Poole had different procedures to follow. The regular dealer in current American books could often obtain subscription books at less than full price. Rare and out-of-print works might be ordered from second-hand dealers who kept them in stock, but it was better and cheaper to buy at auction, usually through an agent who would take a 5 percent commission, although a few auction houses could be trusted to execute a mail bid faithfully. Poole himself, of course, attended a number of important auctions over the years to make his own bids.

During the first six weeks in Chicago, Poole was kept busy preparing book orders, overseeing the arrangement of the new rooms, supervising the staff in the Rookery reading room, and, presumably with assistance, making a card catalog of the 9,300 volumes already on hand. Shortly, the newly ordered books would begin to come from the various dealers.

Poole's paper of advice to library boards covered the subjects of governing authority, proper quarters, and selection and acquisition of books before he mentioned choosing a librarian. This sequence of steps was in accord with his own past practice, for it was only after the first large book order had been placed that he had brought Fletcher to Waterbury or Evans to Indianapolis. Most boards would not be able to command the services of librarians with as much experience as these two. Poole did not believe that a green librarian was any more capable of making wise

selections of books than was the typical new library board. Moreover, in the usual practice of the time, book selection, or at least
the approval of book orders, was a function of the board and not
the librarian, a concept which Poole did not question. He recommended that a new board temporarily employ an expert to make
the selection, as he had been called in to do for various libraries.
In Cincinnati and Chicago he had performed the dual functions
of librarian and of expert, but, then, he had special qualifications.
The sequence and tone of his recommendations suggest that he
thought of the expert as a surrogate for the board rather than for
the librarian.

In his advice about the selection of a librarian, Poole affirmed
his belief in the importance of the position. He warned the boards
not to be deceived into employing any of the "broken down ministers, briefless lawyers, unsuccessful school teachers, and physicians without patients" who would apply.

The business of a librarian is a profession. . . . The same energy, industry, and tact, to say nothing of experience, which insure success in
other avocations are quite as requisite in a librarian as book knowledge. A mere bookworm in charge of a public library . . . is an in-
cubus and a nuisance.

The board should get the best person possible, not limiting itself by the "absurd" notion that the librarian must be selected
from among local residents. It was typical of Poole that he appealed to the common sense of the businessman by pointing out
that this "prejudice" was "one which the individual members of
the board do not observe in conducting their own affairs." The
librarians of larger libraries could suggest candidates among young
men and women being trained in those institutions. He himself
was frequently approached by those responsible for libraries to
suggest candidates and by young librarians to seek his sponsorship.
Before the end of his career, he was so frequently consulted that
he was, in effect, a one-man placement bureau.[6]

The Chicago board, of course, had already solved this problem.
Poole was on the scene long before the new books arrived. By the
middle of March he was ready to move to the new building. Leaving generous room for the expected further acquisitions, he had
the books arranged on the shelves and new shelf lists prepared.

The current American titles then began to come in at a rate exceeding 1,000 a week. As they were received, they were compared with the bills, which were then certified for payment. Each volume was then collated and, if necessary, had its pages cut. By 1876, however, Poole had decided that the expense of collation was not usually justified. Besides, he said, "the young ladies [keep] the novels pretty well collated." [7] The book was then entered in an accession record that gave a complete history, including the author and title, cost, and source. This record, Poole believed, was an absolute necessity, the omission of which would be a serious mistake, especially since it would be discovered, he warned, only too late to correct. This point was one on which he and Winsor, who used order records for the purpose, disagreed.

The next step after accessioning was to catalog the books on cards, a process which Poole felt could never be done to complete satisfaction no matter what system was used. To one librarian who sought his advice, he replied: "Whatever plan you adopt, you will not go far before being sorry you did not adopt some other." [8] To him, the fruitlessness of striving for perfection meant simply that agonizing meticulousness was a waste of time. This did not mean slipshod carelessness, but rather a hardheaded sense of proportion. Certainly, there were "many technical rules for cataloguing which should be thoroughly mastered before one undertakes to catalogue a library," but there was no need to introduce fine details. The purpose of a catalog was "to show what the book is, who is its author . . . what it contains, and its imprint." To that end,

every work must be catalogued under its author or under the first word of the title not an article, in case the author be not known. It must also be catalogued under its subject, or, if it be a work of fiction, under its title. . . . The place and date of publication, the size, the number of volumes, and the accession number must be given in every instance; and cross-references, when necessary, must be made.

Give the essential details which contribute to the purpose, said Poole, but keep it simple: "If a title be long, it is abridged." [9] A catalog, though simple, was not easy to make. Indeed, Poole felt, an inexperienced librarian would find it uneconomical to try to do the work himself. Better to hire, on a temporary basis, thoroughly skilled workers who could make the basic catalog and, at the same time, train the regular librarian to keep it up to the standard which they would establish.

Again, the Chicago library was under no such necessity to bring in outside help. Poole himself, no doubt with assistance from his staff, did the cataloging there in the beginning. He turned out a prodigious amount of work. Between January and June more than 18,000 volumes were cataloged. Of course, as Poole was well aware, this work would not meet with approval from some other librarians. "If . . . the librarian is ambitious to make a contribution to the art of bibliography, he needs different instructions from those which have been given." [10] This variation between his own system and that of others was well known to him, and he stuck to his own ideas. Word came to him that Vickers planned to make a new catalog in Cincinnati "à la Cutter." Poole commented to his friend Evans: "You will be a gray-haired man when that catalogue is done, and what will the Cincinnati public be saying and doing meanwhile?" [11] This comment, incidentally, is Poole's only recorded remark to hint directly that he thought Cutter's Athenaeum catalog picayune and extravagant nonsense, a viewpoint that his general statements about cataloging suggest he held. Since Poole believed that brief, summary cataloging was best, it is not surprising that he was able to do the work quickly.

Cataloging was only one phase of the work of getting the library ready for use. The books had to be marked with stamp or embosser and fitted out with a bookplate. Poole had long since given up the practice he followed at the Mercantile Library of putting the volumes in paper covers. They were apt to strain the hinges of the books, held dirt more easily than leather or even muslin bindings, and made the collection dull, unsightly, and difficult to use.

The books in the Chicago library, being mostly new, did not immediately require much rebinding. In his paper, however, Poole gave the conclusions learned from his experience as tanner and as librarian. Since European binding was better than American and only half as expensive, the Chicago library had its foreign books bound abroad. American commercial binding was so poor that Poole recommended that any library with enough work to justify the step should set up its own bindery. Libraries should not waste their money on ornate and expensive binding but should settle rather for good materials, strong sewing, and competent workmanship. As for leathers, morocco was best, and bark-tanned, unsplit sheep was next, though the more expensive Russia leather might be used for very large volumes. Calf was not durable enough for general library use, and the many cheap leathers made in imitation of better quality should be avoided.

Even after the books were received in new binding, accessioned, collated, stamped, book-plated, and cataloged, they were still not ready. They had to be assigned places on the shelves and a classification scheme devised. The complexity of a classification was a function of the size and type of library; large collections would need more detailed subdivision than small collections, and reference libraries than circulating libraries. For most public libraries a satisfactory classification would be one which included the following classes:

History, biography, voyages and travels, poetry and drama, English miscellanies, English prose fiction, juveniles, polygraphy, collected works of English and American authors, German literature, French literature, Spanish literature . . . language and rhetoric, fine and practical arts, natural history, physics and natural science, political and social science, education, religion, law, medicine, and serials.

Each subject should then be further subdivided. History, for example, would be broken down by country and by period; biography into collected and individual; fine arts into sculpture, painting, drawing, and architecture; and similarly through the various broad subjects. Poole did not spell out the classification in detail. He viewed classification, as he did other matters of library operation, as a practical problem to be solved in a particular situation. Reclassification as a library grew was an inevitable necessity. Neither his own nor, he asserted, "any other plan will provide for indefinite expansion." [12] Granting the assumption that periodic reclassification was a necessity, detailed elaboration of a theoretically logical classification was not merely unnecessary but a waste of effort.

Once a classification had been made, it was necessary to devise a system of call numbers which would relate the books to the shelves. Poole still did not repudiate the idea of a notation which referred to specific shelves for a reference library like the Athenaeum. Indeed, a system which tied a volume not simply to a particular shelf but to fixed order on that shelf was still sufficiently usual for Poole to describe it in detail in his paper. For a circulating library, the system he preferred was more flexible, though still a form of fixed location. Under this plan, Poole designated each case of shelves by a letter of the alphabet, but, instead of numbering the shelves and assigning each book to a particular one, he used for the call number only the letter of the case and a serial number from one to whatever numerical limit was required for the books which could be contained in the case. Thus, within each case, the books could be moved freely so long as they were kept in numerical order. As at the Athenaeum, the subject arrangement was obtained by assigning particular subjects to specific cases. Although Poole did not say so, it is clear that, in Chicago, there were too many books in any one class to be contained in a single case of shelves. Evidently, a single letter of the shelf notation referred to a group of cases. Under each subject, subdivision was provided by reserving large blocks of numbers for each subclass, thus making it possible to put new accessions into their proper subject places. The task of estimating how many numbers to leave unused for future additions was the most difficult problem of all, requiring considerable wisdom and judgment and even then doomed to being unsatisfactory. Fortunately, however, the inevitable rearrangement and reclassification would give the opportunity to correct the difficulties.

With a card catalog made, a classification scheme devised and applied, and shelf marks assigned, the final step was to prepare a shelf list. Under the call number for each book was listed the author, a brief title, the number of volumes, and the number of copies.

At this point, the Chicago library did not have its basic collection near enough to completion to warrant printing a catalog. In a small library, Poole thought it sufficient to make written lists to post in the building; for a library as large as that in Chicago, such an expedient would not be feasible. Poole hit upon the idea of printing a "finding list" using an adaptation of the shelf list as copy. Thus, the patrons would have available, for use in the library or at home, a list of the collection arranged under subjects and with call numbers. An index to the various subdivisions facilitated the use of the rudimentary classed catalog. Under each subject and subdivision, books were listed alphabetically, usually by author, but, in the case of biography, by the name of the person whose life was narrated.[13]

This ingenious solution did not entirely satisfy Poole. He continued to believe that a printed catalog was the ideal and ultimately an essential. He was adamant in his disapproval of Winsor's decision in 1871 to undertake to print cards and set up a public card catalog. Of course, Poole had a card catalog for official use, always kept ready for the time when it could be sent off to be used as copy for the printed catalog. But he evidently thought it unwise to put the only copy of such a valuable record into the hands of the public. Readers in Chicago could get information from this catalog, but only through the mediation of an attendant, who, in later years, was kept very busy indeed.

Never again was Poole to print a library catalog, but he gave his advice on the subject to library boards. Pointing out the great expense of printing and the rapid obsolescence of a printed catalog, he recommended brief entries, an uncomplicated arrangement, and simple printing. Since the major part of the cost would be for composition rather than paper, ink, and other components of the physical product, he urged the use of large, clear type. He had once chided Winsor for using small type which had forced Poole "to buy a pair of spectacles and become an old man before my time." [14] It would be better to use an ordinary octavo page and legible brevier type, as he had done at the Mercantile Library and in Cincinnati and as his protégés had done in Indianapolis, Waterbury, and Newton. As for the plan of arrangement, Poole, with a fine disregard for leading exponents of the classed catalog, like Ezra Abbot of Harvard and Jacob Schwartz of the New York Apprentices Library, simply described the dictionary catalog as "the one which is now almost universally used, and is preferable to the classified plan." [15]

The Chicago library had no printed catalog, and many of its

books had not been received, but much work had been done. On March 16, 1874, the move to the new quarters began. Despite the prodigious amount of work under way, the directors would never be satisfied until the institution was open to borrowers. Poole continued to believe that the opening of a new library should wait until a substantial collection was ready. But in the face of the board's insistence, he accepted their decision to begin to lend books. On May 1, the new library opened its doors to borrowers.

The new quarters consisted of a reading room separated by a circulation counter from the library space. Poole was so certain of the wisdom of closed shelves in a public library that he did not even mention it directly. In the library portion of the quarters, the wooden shelves were placed at right angles to the walls and away from them so as to allow free passage for the attendants and cross light for the shelves not directly in front of the windows. The shelves were limited to a height which "a person of ordinary stature" [16] (meaning a six-footer like Poole) could reach. Holes in the uprights made the shelves adjustable, and a uniform length made them interchangeable.

The books lent across the circulation counter were recorded on slips that were filed under the date of loan and arranged under each date by the borrower's number. Since these files were simply accounts with the borrowers and not a means of recording the whereabouts of every book not on the shelves, it was possible to divide the file into separate units. The time-consuming part of loan transactions, Poole said, was the return of books, not their loan. In order to reduce the congestion and to speed up the process, separate loan files were maintained for men, for women, and for juvenile borrowers. This separation had the additional benefit of allowing certain attendants to become especially familiar with the parts of the book collection of interest to different groups, with better service possible for each group.

With a large and transient population served by a public library in a metropolis, it was important to have careful identification and registration of each patron before permitting him to borrow. First, it was necessary that the board adopt a set of rules defining the terms under which persons were eligible to register and specifying the conditions of use. A borrower was required to make a cash deposit or, better, to secure on a guarantee form the signature of a responsible person who would agree to indemnify the library for any fines or losses resulting from the borrower's use. In order to weed out the names of those who had moved and to keep the guarantees viable, Chicago adopted in 1877 a two-year limit on the validity of a registration. The basic records were registration books containing, on each page, a printed pledge to abide by the library's rules and a series of prenumbered lines; the registrant, by his signature on the indicated line, affirmed the pledge. The number of the line which he signed then became his borrower's number and was noted on his library card. Indexes were prepared giving an alphabetical record of registrants and also an alphabetical list of guarantors with a notation of the names of the persons for whom they stood responsible. Thus, if a guarantor reneged on his pledge, all the cards for which he was responsible could be canceled. With the preliminaries performed, the patron was eligible to borrow.

The number who came to the library to register and then to borrow was tremendous. Within two months after the May 1 opening, more than 5,000 had registered with the library and others were coming in at the rate of 100 per day. Circulation climbed steadily; within nine weeks 800 volumes per day, on the average, were being lent. This figure exceeded that of the public libraries in Boston and Cincinnati even though both had much larger collections. Poole took pride in pointing out Chicago's prosperity:

This position, there is every reason to believe, it will hold, and improve upon. . . . It is probable that no library in the country, whatever may [b]e its age or size, is at the present time circulating so many books. With no competing library in the city, and with a population of nearly half a million looking to it for reading, it seems now impossible to fix any limit to the use which will be made of its books when the shelves are fully supplied.[17]

The Chicago Public Library was, Poole felt, on the right track. In the future the acquisition and service program would have to be vastly expanded. Convinced though he was of the appropriateness of fiction, he was also very conscious of the need to provide the resources for scholarship. He told Winsor how keenly he himself felt the lack of research collections. "You can hardly conceive how a literary man is cramped out here from the want of books. This is the one drawback I feel in my residence in the West." [18] Only by "providing the necessary appliances which literary men must have," he warned in his annual report, would it be possible to accomplish the goal of "cultivating a literature, and a popular literary taste in the West." Yet the future was hopeful. The progress already made was "an earnest that the literary wants of Chicago, the great metropolis of the Northwest, are to be met." The city, he predicted, was destined to have an "immense" public library which, in the lifetime of persons then living, would occupy "acres of ground." With such tremendous growth inevitable, he thought it fortunate that construction of a building was not yet possible. Chicago should not yet try to make final building plans. "A location too narrow, and a plan of building too contracted and ill adapted for the future, might be the result." [19] Such had been the fate of other city libraries, including Boston, as Poole was doubtless not sorry to point out. Nor would branch libraries eliminate the need for a great main library. These developments would have to wait for years, but the beginnings were most promising. To one correspondent Poole wrote: "Chicago means to have a large Library, and we shall bring it about." [20]

After years in Cincinnati and a short time in Chicago, Poole was becoming accustomed to his life away from Massachusetts. To hear him tell it, the move had been the best thing he had ever done. And, if his comments sometimes had the slight flavor of sour grapes, it was nevertheless quite true that the West for him was the land of opportunity. His salary had risen quickly. More than that, his field of service was expanded. He wrote to Winsor in 1872: "There are new libraries springing up all over the west, and I am a good deal consulted in their organization." [21] At times his bank account was helped by the consultation, but, perhaps even more important than the financial rewards, there was the satisfaction which he could take in being the leading librarian in a great and expanding section of the nation. He had told Evans to get away from "the shadow of Winsor, Cutter and Abbot" where one "must do everything as they do it, or you don't understand your business. . . . Nobody can make a mark in a library in the vicinity of Boston." An ambitious librarian must get "far enough away to be independent, and to be a man." [22] There can be no doubt that Poole, as the foremost librarian of the region, was indeed "a good deal consulted," nor that his advice had influence in determining the course of public librarianship in the West.

Personally, too, he was becoming a part of his new homeland. His natural brash, blunt, and hearty manner had more the tone of the Westerner than of the cold New Englander in any case. Even in his ailments he had taken on the flavor of the outland which was becoming his home. "I have become very much of a western man, and can shake with chills, if need be, as well as the best of them. I am better now than I have been for three months, and am taking quinine." [23] Though tropical diseases—Poole said his trouble was bilious fever—were beginning to recede somewhat in the upper Middle West, they were still common enough complaints not to be treated too seriously. By their nature, the sufferer was apt to improve periodically even if nothing special were done for him, and, presumably, Poole was also getting better care. In June he had gone to Massachusetts to bring back his family. He established them in a house just south of the old University of Chicago. Poole could now settle down to a routine familiar to him from Athenaeum days, commuting each day on the train from Fairview Station near the University. Alternatively, he could take the Cottage Grove streetcar, but it was not so quick nor so pleasant as his usual trip by train. He was coming to be a confirmed Chicagoan in his habits and also in his willingness, not new to him, to look to the future with confidence.

In other ways as well, Poole began to make a place for himself in the life of the city during 1874. Two ventures, collaterally related to his work, took his attention. In the fall, he accepted editorship of a new literary journal sponsored by W. B. Keen, Cooke and Company, the library's American book dealer, primarily as a means of publicizing new books, and "after the 2d or 3d number wrote all the critical notices of books and other matter in it." [24] *The Owl* consisted mainly of brief annotations of twenty or thirty new books in each monthly issue. It continued publication until 1876, and, by virtue of its literary nature, was a spiritual ancestor of Francis Fisher Browne's *The Dial,* which gained a place as an important journal and one to which Poole contributed regularly in the years to follow.[25]

A second enterprise was Poole's active participation in the founding of the Chicago Literary Club. In this group, which came to be one of the foremost cultural organizations in the city, Poole played an enthusiastic part. To him it was a reflection of a kind of equality and democracy which was typical of the West and not to be found in Boston.

Boston is an older community. There are too many tape-rolls of respectability running down through seven or eight generations; and it is impossible in Boston to have a society of this kind consisting of more than a dozen or fifteen members, because they don't belong to each other. Now, in the Far West we are on a glorious equality—and that is one reason why I like the West. We all stand on a general footing.[26]

Designed to be "one place in Chicago where money did not count," [27] the club included many of the most alert men of the city, among whom Poole found some of his fast friends. Eliphalet Wickes Blatchford, later trustee of the Newberry Library; Francis Fisher Browne, editor at that time of *The Lakeside Monthly* and later of *The Dial;* Franklin MacVeagh, wholesale grocer, active citizen, member of the Newberry's board, and Secretary of the Treasury under Taft; Edward Gay Mason, lawyer and avocational historian; Daniel Lewis Shorey, lawyer and member of the Chicago Public Library's board; Horace White, the editor of the *Tribune*—all were among his special friends. Poole served on several club committees and, from 1879 to 1880, as its president.

As a newcomer to the city, Poole did not participate in the preliminary arrangements of the Literary Club, but he was elected at the first formal meeting of the club and began his regular attendance the next week. His experience with the Cincinnati Literary Club gave him background that was helpful as the matter of a constitution was discussed. A three-man committee produced a document which Poole described as "the most gorgeous piece of literary composition that ever came under my notice; tropes, figures, metaphors, and rhetorical fireworks chased each other with dazzling brilliancy." [28] The earnestness of the constitutional committee made criticism difficult, but finally one member got up the courage to move the omission of the preamble. After that motion had been carried unanimously, with the abstention of the committee, Horace White broke the embarrassing situation by proposing the omission of all of the document *except* the preamble. The members could then proceed to make a sensible basic law for the club. Poole's friend Mason recalled:

He brought with him the constitution of the Cincinnati Literary Club, and although we used jokingly to allude to his quotations from it as the "Cincinnati Platform" and to speak of its printed order of exercises as "Poole's Index," we all realized that his experience in that association was of great value to us.[29]

Poole was very proud of his membership in the club and sensitive to any suggestion that, having joined only after several informal meetings of the organizers, he was not really a founder. He was so predictably touchy on the subject that his friends delighted in baiting him about it. Not unaware that he was being teased, he was still not willing to let the point pass. Mason went on:

He used to assert with great positiveness that he was truly one of the founders of this club; and if it was necessary, in order to establish that fact, to hold that the meeting of April 7, 1874, *preceded* that of March 13 of the same year, he was ready to maintain that position.[30]

And, if required to do so, he would no doubt have defended his thesis plausibly, for he was a remarkable debater whose favorite device was to take his opponent's strongest argument and turn it against him. When Winsor called the Cincinnati building "absurd," Poole responded that, not willing to concede the criticism in the case of his own building, he would agree that Winsor's library was indeed "absurd," as he proceeded to point out in some detail.[31] In 1876, when he presented a full-dress argument for fiction in public libraries before the Philadelphia conference of librarians, he took the charge of falseness and turned it to his own account by an extended discussion of the essential truth of great novels, as contrasted with the many errors of supposedly factual history or science, concluding with the rhetorical question: "Shall we say that in literature and science there is nothing true but fiction and the pure mathematics?" [32]

Banter and playful debate added spice to the meetings of the club, but the gatherings were devoted to serious consideration of substantive topics, not necessarily limited to literary matters.

The stimulation of the frequent meetings added zest to the lives of those who belonged and made others want to join.

For Poole, participation in the organization was closely in line with his professional life. As in Cincinnati, his opportunity to associate on a basis of social friendship with many leading men of the city was a considerable help in his work as librarian. The Chicago Literary Club had a restricted membership to which new recruits came only by invitation after vote by the attending members. Thus, not all directors of the public library were members, but some of them were. Shorey, in particular, who became president of the library's board in 1875 and remained until 1880, was Poole's special friend and near neighbor.

Poole was successful in making a place for himself and for his library in the community, but his great hopes for the future were not realized for some years. Just as the library was getting under way, unfortunate developments in the city's politics seriously damaged the library's program and even threatened its existence.

The library had begun with sympathetic backing from the city administration under Mayor Joseph Medill. Although the library board had broad powers to act on its own, it was dependent upon the city government in two crucial areas: its own membership and the annual decision on the rate of the tax levy. In connection with the appointment of board members, the library had no particular problem; the several annual reports reflect the actions of men who were, in general, conscientiously devoted to the interests of the library enterprise. The tax rate was another matter. The Illinois law, which set a maximum library tax of one mill on the property valuation for most communities, limited the return to one fifth of a mill for cities above 100,000 population—in effect, only Chicago. The drastic cut was not entirely unreasonable, since a small community needed a high rate in order to produce the minimum number of dollars to support any library at all; for a large city like Chicago, even the lower rate represented substantial sums of money, anticipated to run between $50,000 and $60,000, an amount which would increase with the growth of the city. The library backers did expect, however, that the city council would assess at the full rate allowed. One other important feature of the financial arrangements was that the council did not make a dollar appropriation but merely set a tax rate. The library's income, therefore, was dependent upon the success of the city in collecting the money. The result was that the library never received the amount estimated for a particular year, since the estimate assumed complete collection. Moreover, as the years went by, delinquent taxes grew to very substantial amounts. In June, 1876, for example, the library fund showed an uncollected balance above $61,000, one third of the total due the library since its beginnings. This ostensible credit made the library's accounts look much more affluent than they really were.

Under the Medill regime the levy was set at or near the maximum during the first two years of the library's existence. But when the mayor ordered the police to enforce the law closing saloons on Sunday, he was opposed by an unlikely coalition between the Germans and the Irish, whose primary bond was the deep conviction that whisky on Sunday was more important than any petty governmental matter. The resulting People's Party was swept into office. Its policy of retrenchment combined with flagrant corruption left little money for such a luxury as a public library. The result was that, just as the library was getting under way with brilliant success, its budget was drastically reduced. Although the effect was somewhat cushioned by windfalls as delinquent tax collections brought in extra money each year, the library was hard hit.

All book purchases were stopped for a time, a number of periodical subscriptions were canceled, and less expensive quarters were rented. This move was not particularly damaging to the library, but the dearth of new books had its bad effects not simply in the lack of the latest titles, but in an inability to supply the demand for duplicate copies of titles which the library already owned. It would have been much quicker to give a patron the first book he requested than to look for several before finding a suitable substitute. As a result, long lines of borrowers began to develop around the delivery counters, and, what was worse, even when a patron's turn came, it was all too frequently impossible to find any book at all to satisfy him. Thus, at a time when it would have been desirable to economize on staff, it was necessary to hire even more help to meet the extra burdens imposed by a shortage of books.

These difficulties were enough to give Poole a new view of library legislation. The tax rate, he said, should not be subject to discretionary changes: "The income of a library, be it larger or smaller, should be uniform, and not subject to the vote of a department of the city government which is liable to have fits of liberality and economy." [33] He evidently did not consider at the time the argument that a library is properly subject to the same economic and political processes which regulate appropriations to other branches of the municipal government. Not long after, however, he reconsidered his position on this point, concluding that artificial protection for the library was by no means certain insurance. "Public appreciation of these institutions, based on the work they are doing is, after all, the only sure guaranty that they will be liberally supported, enlarged, and cherished." [34]

Public appreciation of the Chicago library was evident. Despite the shortage in the book collection, the number of registered borrowers rose in 1874–75 to over 23,000. Almost exactly 400,000 volumes were lent; on a single day, 2,452 volumes were issued. When it is considered that ordinarily only one book could be taken at a time, the figure becomes even more impressive. This early experience clearly demonstrated, said Poole, "a famishing need of books in this community." [35]

Despite the popularity of the library, the city administration was not moved. During 1874–75, the appropriation was only $25,000, less than half that of previous years. Worse, the budget for 1875–76 omitted the library entirely. Although, after vigorous protest by the library board and the city's newspapers, an appropriation was made, it was still only at the starvation level of the previous year. Salaries were cut by 10 percent, subscriptions were canceled, and once again book purchases were sharply curtailed. The financial position of the city became so desperate that payment of salaries was suspended for three months in the spring of 1876, and bills were left unpaid. Part of the difficulty came as a result of a business depression which curtailed tax collection, but the corrupt city administration bore a major share of the blame. The library board president, Thomas Hoyne, resigned his position in order to be free to lead the "good government" forces, at whose head he was elected mayor in a write-in campaign. Although his election was invalidated by the courts, the reform victories in the city council stood.

Even after this victory, the city's finances were so badly tangled that no increase could be allowed for the library for 1876–77. Salaries were cut a second time, making the total reduction 25 percent. Again, only a few books could be bought, but the use of the library remained at a high level. Services were continued and even expanded. With the move to new and less expensive quarters in 1875, the reference books were moved from the reading room to space behind the railing of the library. During the next year, this service was expanded by the provision of additional tables and chairs, and, by the middle of 1876, Poole was speaking of it as a reference department. New editions of the finding list were published, with the edition of February, 1876, introducing a new feature. Up to that time the lists had been produced by the library and sold at thirty cents a copy. Now a local printer agreed to print the lists himself and sell them for only ten cents in return for the privilege of selling advertising space in the booklet. The library was thus relieved of any cost in producing its lists, and the patrons got them at a reduced price.

Although the financial difficulties of the library stemmed mainly from the city's poverty, an event which occurred in Italy on April 4, 1876, brought to the minds of some the idea that public support of a library was no longer necessary. With the death of the last surviving daughter of Walter Loomis Newberry, the city of Chicago was assured of a generously endowed public library. Although the library could not be started until after the termination of Mrs. Newberry's life interest in her husband's estate, it was now a certainty, and the prospect suggested to some that the city should not invest much money in a library of its own.

Poole could not have agreed less. To him the Newberry bequest opened the way to the creation of a great reference collection with resources greater than any other in the nation. The prospect was that it would assemble a magnificent research collection unequaled in the United States. Its existence should not, however, reduce the importance of the public library but, rather, should free it to concentrate upon its function as the principal circulating library of the city. "No one library, however large its resources, can meet the many sided wants of a metropolitan community with a population of half a million." [36] If there was in Poole's description the hint of a chauvinistic boast that Chicago, even above New York, now had the resources to create a great national reference library, his pride was surely pardonable. His statesmanlike vision of the place of the Newberry Library in the nation and in the community reflected a remarkable devotion to the cause of librarianship in general. There was no trace of jealousy that another institution might rise to overshadow his own, nor of any wish to compete with it. No matter how much credit is due to others in Chicago, the tone which the city's library leader set in 1876 must surely have been a major factor in creating the atmosphere which, with all its faults and deficiencies, was to put the libraries of that community in the vanguard of cooperative planning and action in the United States. If some in Chicago saw in the Newberry legacy an excuse for the municipal government to cast off its responsibilities, Poole conceived of it as an opportunity for an expanded service which would make Chicago the literary capital of the nation. The dream was never entirely fulfilled, and, so far as the Newberry Library was concerned, its formal establishment was to wait for more than a decade.

It was welcome news that the people of Chicago had the prospect of a great and wealthy institution, but the public library still had to struggle along with meager resources. During the next few years, the brilliant start deteriorated into a holding operation to keep the library going until economic recovery and an untangling of the city's finances would permit a restoration of funds. Not until 1879–80 was much of a beginning made. Meanwhile, the book collection was replenished in numbers so small as to fail to keep pace with its depletion. The result was a decline in circulation which became progressively worse as the book collection dwindled, finally reaching a low point of about 300,000 during 1879–80 before the new books bought in that year could begin to have their effect. With such financial stringency, few innovations were possible. To save money, service was curtailed by closing the circulation department at night. Although, after a few months, the board decided to reopen for two nights a week, it was not until the middle of 1879 that a full restoration of night service was possible.

Despite all these difficulties, Poole's annual reports remained optimistic. Poole complained of the lack of funds, but always in terms which pointed to the evident needs and desires of the people of Chicago. He spoke of the great opportunities to be seized if funds were made available and appealed to the pride of the city to make the public library the leader which the city itself aspired to be in the nation. Poole's leadership in library affairs extended even beyond the city. Indeed, for libraries throughout the Middle West, he served as a guide. He said that "committees and librarians from nearly every thriving city and town in the Northwest" had visited his library or had written for information or advice. This was a kind of inquiry to which Poole "regarded it a duty as well as pleasure to reply." [37] He also took a leading part in national library affairs, largely through the newly founded American Library Association.

VII. The American
Library Association

The American Library Association occupied an important place in Poole's life during the eighteen years from its founding in 1876 to his death in 1894. Year after year, his professional life in his own library was spiced by a trip to meet his friends and colleagues at the association's conference. He never failed to attend its official meetings during those years. He played a leading part in association affairs, serving from the beginning on its committees and as a vice-president and later for two years as its president. The American Library Association offered him a platform from which he expressed his ideas about librarianship. Under its sponsorship he was enabled to complete the monumental third edition of his *Index* and its supplements. In addition to the professional contributions which the association made to his life and those which he made to its life, the association gave him much personal pleasure.

Poole was said never to be so happy as when he went off by train on one of his regular trips to attend the association's conference. Founded in Philadelphia in 1876, the association held its meetings in the eastern cities of New York, Boston, and Washington during the early years. It then went west to Cincinnati, returned east to Buffalo and Lake George, and then moved to Milwaukee. In later years it met at the Thousand Islands, in St. Louis, and in the White Mountains. Finally, in 1891, the members took the bold step of holding the meeting in California, and it was Poole's delight to join the excursion train on its wide-ranging journey through the West, feted at every stop. After a peripatetic meeting in Lakewood, New Jersey, Baltimore, and Washington in 1892, the association met in Poole's home city of Chicago—the last meeting he attended. Without the need and desire to go to these meetings, it is doubtful that he would have been able to travel so widely, especially because his library was one of the few at the time which paid its librarian's expenses. The association was indirectly responsible for Poole's one trip to Europe, for the success of the 1876 meeting inspired a group of English librarians to call an international conference in 1877. Poole joined the party that went abroad for the meeting, visiting libraries in Scotland and England before the conference in London and traveling to Paris after it. Throughout the years, Poole's part in the American Library Association was the source of great professional and personal satisfaction to him.

Poole enjoyed attending conferences. He cherished the memory of the 1853 meeting, where he began his warm friendship with Lloyd Pearsall Smith, hereditary librarian of the Library Company of Philadelphia. The first word of the 1876 conference, however, was greeted by Poole with considerable suspicion. Out of a clear sky, he received a telegram asking his endorsement of a call to a conference in Philadelphia in conjunction with the Centennial celebration of that year. The telegram is traditionally the bearer of bad news, and this one clearly upset him. He refused to be stampeded and replied by letter that he would need to know more about the sponsorship before lending his name to the movement. His investigations did not allay his suspicions. He found that the leading backers were Frederick Leypoldt, editor and publisher of *Publishers' Weekly*, and one Melvil Dewey. Leypoldt's journal was the spokesman for the book trade, which, Poole felt, had recently shown itself hostile to libraries by adopting a limit of 20 percent on the discount to be given libraries. Although Poole had been successful in circumventing the restriction, he was outraged by the book trade's "ring" and humiliated by the expedients to which he had been forced in order to get around the discount limit. He wrote to Winsor: "I hate the idea that libraries must buy books in back streets and dives, and not in open day, as if ours were not an honest business." [1] This disagreement with publishers made Poole wary of a proposal made by the editor of the publishers' trade journal. Equally, the reports about Dewey were not encouraging. This young man, who had been serving as assistant librarian at Amherst College, was concentrating his attention that summer on three of his interests: simplified spelling, metric reform, and libraries. In each case, he promoted a conference in Philadelphia and started an association. Ainsworth Rand Spofford at the Library of Congress wrote to Poole that a Massachusetts Congressman who knew Amherst well said that Dewey was "a tremendous talker, and a little of an old maid." [2] Poole warned Winsor that there were *"axes to be ground"* and concluded: "It won't pay for you and me to attend that barbecue." [3] Winsor, however, had received a visit from Dewey and was evidently impressed, for he decided to join the enterprise. Once Winsor agreed to accept the chairmanship of the organizing committee, Poole was satisfied and agreed to join with his friend Smith of Philadelphia to form the three-man committee. Soon Poole was writing letters of friendly advice to Dewey.

In later years, Dewey accused Poole of opposing the holding of the conference and the formation of the association which grew from it. As a result, the idea of Poole's opposition has become a part of the literature of librarianship. Dewey's purpose in making the statement was to strengthen his case when Poole opposed some of his later projects. Dewey's reasoning went that the conference had been his idea, that Poole had opposed it, and that the outcome of the idea had been a successful association. By parallel, Poole was opposed to Dewey's new idea of the moment; therefore, this idea too must be a good one. Poole heard these remarks without protest for a time and then struck back:

The conference idea has never had a warmer friend, from the start, than W.F.P. or one that has more persistently maintained his interest in it, attended every one of its meetings, and contributed, as well as he could, to all its proceedings. You have in mind some hesitation of mine in giving in my name when it was asked by telegraph. I then had no information on which I could base an opinion as to the scheme. I am not a person to go blindly into a scheme until I know who is behind it. I never expressed any opposition to the conference idea *provided* it was backed by such men as Winsor, Cutter, and others in whom I had confidence. When that fact was brought to my notice, I sailed in, and have done my level best. To have taken any other course, would not have been my way of doing business.[4]

Clearly, Poole's defense is a fair statement of the case. He was not opposed to a conference; on the contrary, he had pleasant memories of the 1853 meeting and enjoyed such gatherings. It is also true, however, that he was opposed to a conference controlled by men with private interests to promote; he was in favor of a conference controlled by disinterested men of integrity. Once the sponsorship question was settled, he joined heartily into the work.

The Philadelphia meeting was a happy beginning to the association's activities. Attended by many of the country's leading librarians, it set a precedent for hard work and wide-ranging discussion of all aspects of librarianship. Book selection and acquisition, binding and preparation, cataloging and classification, book storage and circulation, relations with governing boards and patrons, reference services, library legislation, buildings, and administration—all these subjects and others as well were discussed both in broad terms of policy and in detail at the association's conferences during the next years. Poole spoke on most of these subjects from time to time, most frequently on book selection, library legislation, and buildings, and to a lesser extent on indexing, library cooperation, and service to schools. He often read prepared papers, and he participated freely in the discussions of his own and other papers.

Poole was notably successful in reaching his audience without letting the paper before him become a barrier. One who was present in 1876 described the scene as he remembered it:

We have before us, as Mr. Poole rises to speak, the towering figure of a six-footer, about fifty-five years of age, and rather loosely built, with powerful shoulders. Like Mr. Winsor he wears a beard, but unlike Mr. Winsor, he has somewhat Dundreary-like side-whiskers. These are of a sandy color, as is also his hair. His eyes are a noticeable feature of his countenance, and they decidedly contribute to the kindly expression which his face at all times wears. Rising to his feet, and adjusting his eyeglasses, he gazes in a benignant manner upon the audience before proceeding to read from his notes. A slight impediment in his manner of speaking, and his occasional departure from the written notes, to take his audience into his confidence, so to speak, give him one of the most winning expressions possible. He is plainly a man with whom the joy of living will always count for more than mechanical routine. His mellow view of life is something which imperceptibly communicates itself to those who are brought into contact with him.[5]

Successful though Poole proved in any circumstance as a public speaker, his real forte was informal discussion and debate. In the association meetings, his readiness to speak became the subject of a standing joke. The pattern was set in 1877, when Winsor, as presiding officer, invited him to give his views on the best ways to recruit members for the association:

As I was going along the street, I noticed that the shutters of a fashionable shop were closed; and upon my inquiry whether the house had failed, I was informed that they had simply closed for a few days "preparatory to the fall opening." Mr. Poole, who is a member of a literary club at Chicago, has been sitting very quietly, thinking over the subject, I suppose, and I have no doubt he has been preparing himself for a grand opening. (Laughter) [6]

But, if there was laughter, it was neither ridicule nor scorn. The meetings were small, and, serious though the participants might be, lightness and banter were not missing. As the members became acquainted over the years, some fell into special roles. Winsor was the dignified and poised moderator, not holding himself above discussion but never joining the rough and tumble of debate. So considerable was his prestige that no one dared argue with him directly, though the members were not afraid to say that their opinions differed from his. Cutter was the quiet and gentle onlooker who took a leading part in the discussion only when he was called upon to deliver a paper or a report. Not that he refrained from participation; he might make comments or even carry on a colloquy from time to time. But generally he entered late into a debate, quietly going to the heart of the issue as his keen and logical mind indicated it to him. Time after time a final action would turn out to coincide with the position which Cutter, almost unnoticed, had taken. Dewey, as secretary of the association, was frequently required to make an official announcement or to explain the background of a recommendation. He did not stay out of the discussions, but the extent of his participation was, especially in the early years, decidedly less than might be expected from the prominent place he held in the association. Quite clearly, however, reports from one or another of the committees made recommendations in whose formulation he had played an active part. Dewey was astute enough to know that he

William Frederick Poole, about 1876

could get his way better by allowing others to advocate it rather than by always taking the lead himself.

Poole's role in the association's meetings was that of the elder statesman who had seen much and learned much. He is said to have remarked once that "he thought he knew all that was worth knowing about librarianship." [7] He was used to public meetings and at ease before them. One particularly striking example of this poise was his appearance at the conference of librarians in London. In the easy manner of an accomplished speaker, he adapted his remarks to his audience, using British examples to illustrate his points and referring by name to various librarians who were there; when costs were mentioned, he gave them in British currency. His ease was not blandness, however, for he had decided opinions and was not reluctant to express them. If the discussion dragged, a presiding officer—usually Winsor in the early years—could call on Poole, confident that he would have something to say. When the debate centered on a subject of his interest, Poole did not hesitate to state his position, nor was he abashed if he found himself in the minority. Indeed, a chance of controversy added to the zest. With all his willingness to speak, he could be silent as well. It is striking to see how frequently he sat back quietly while others disagreed strongly with positions which he had taken. It was as though he felt that, having stated his opinion, he had no need to reiterate it or to refute criticism. He had given his views; now let others give theirs. His remarkable facility for clarity of statement meant that seldom did disagreement arise from misunderstanding. For all the jokes about his readiness to talk, his words were not discounted, even when the vote went against his views. He had dignity, confidence, and self-respect, and others respected him.

With Winsor, Poole's disagreements were never on matters which came to a vote. Indeed, the two men were in substantial agreement on most issues. Poole never accepted Winsor's abandonment of accession books and printed catalogs or his advocacy of low-ceilinged book stacks. But neither man was one to try to impose his own views on others. The disagreements were strongly stated and the conclusions then left for each to reach on his own. A healthy rivalry and a friendly competition existed between the two men. Poole never seems to have resented the fact that he was Winsor's second in the association during the early years. The Bostonian was chosen president at the Philadelphia meeting and held the place for ten years. When he finally declined reelection, Poole succeeded him as a matter of course. Although Poole's refusal to serve a third term might be interpreted as a rebuke to Winsor, there is no evidence of a complaint from Poole on this score. Poole delighted in twitting Winsor about the deficiencies of Boston's building. When a Bostonian visited Chicago and commented that he had never seen such a well-run library, Poole said gleefully: "Winsor will like to hear of this." [8] Even when Winsor, in an unaccountable lapse from his usual urbanity, spoke at a public meeting in Chicago of the fact that the librarianship there had been offered to Poole only after he himself had declined it, Poole did not react. One looks in vain for any indication of petty jealousy or resentment. Poole's manner with Winsor was open and hearty. Though the aloof Bostonian was not one to reciprocate in kind, he evidently cherished affection and respect for Poole. It was undoubtedly Winsor's backstage manipulation which won for Poole the place as Winsor's successor to the presidency of the American Historical Association.

With Melvil Dewey, Poole's relationship was quite different. Their initial difficulty over the sponsorship of the Philadelphia conference was soon forgotten, and, at that meeting, they got along well. Dewey's energy and ability were apparent to all, as much to Poole as to anyone. And, in Philadelphia, Poole was the wise and experienced veteran who could look with amused tolerance upon the impetuous youth, thirty years his junior. As the years passed, however, disagreements between the two men were regular occurrences.

These disagreements were of much more than personal importance, for they reflected fundamental differences of approach to librarianship. In the long run, Dewey's influence—wielded through the machinery of the association, the pages of the *Library Journal,* and the classes of the Albany library school—prevailed. The resulting standardization of method conferred many benefits on American librarianship but also had its drawbacks in its rigidity and dogmatism. Dewey introduced system and order but often at the expense of life and creativity. American librarianship can thank Dewey for training scores of young librarians to work in the many new libraries of the country, but it can also call him to account for encouraging the bloodless slave to rules, whose public image was all too often not a caricature but a true portrait. The disagreements between Poole and Dewey had at their root Poole's protests against Dewey's efforts to use the association as a vehicle to promote his own ideas and to impose them on other librarians. The differences reflected the basic philosophies of the two men.

Dewey constantly sought to reach final answers. In his view, the ideal was to codify library practice so that all librarians everywhere should do things the same way, "the best" way. Although he made many a bow to the need for individual variation and to the freedom of each to do as he pleased, his whole approach was that of a man who believed it was possible to discover the best book, the best size of catalog card, the best way to do anything. Once the best was discovered, only a foolish man would fail to be guided by it.

Poole was one who believed that circumstances altered cases. In the organization and administration of a library, he found zest and excitement. The Biblical injunction, "the letter killeth, but the spirit giveth life," is an appropriate description of his approach to library problems. He was practical and could express his opinions dogmatically, but one of his most prominent characteristics was the spirit which he brought to librarianship, a zest which made his own work satisfying and which inspired his associates. It was not to him a matter of deciding "the best" way. Each community was different from every other, in size, in interests, in local habits. Their libraries must therefore be different also.

Poole's first protest on this matter came in 1877, when he earned for himself the editorial description as "the Martin Luther of the Conference." [9] He agreed that the group might express an opinion on a matter such as the advisability of accession books, but he thought the question of capitalization of book titles in cataloging was a matter of personal taste. He himself would not feel bound to follow either recommendation and would continue to capitalize words in book titles "until we get ready to write a small 'I' for the personal pronoun." [10] In such matters, Dewey was willing to abandon any conventional forms for the sake of simplicity, even going so far as to spell his own name "Dui" for several years. Poole was actually something of a progressive in spelling, in that he advocated the use of American as opposed to English spelling in such words as "center" and the good old American "plow," but he was not at all a radical. He strongly resented Dewey's practice as secretary in abbreviating names in the reports of the association's meetings. "My name is William, not a W and a colon. My name is Frederick, not an F and a colon." Dewey, however, was secretary and in control, so that even these remarks were reported as having been made by "Mr. W: F: Poole." [11]

Dewey's position meant that he could stifle effective action to control his propensity for seeking association endorsement of his personal ideas. In 1889 he found Cutter, Poole, and Winsor united in a determination to clip his wings by the passage of a resolution opposing the taking of votes to endorse systems, procedures, opinions, or plans. Faced with so powerful a coalition, Dewey managed to get the resolution referred to a committee for a later report which became lost in postponements and inaction, a fate which one of Dewey's own schemes would never have met.

Dewey's tendency to treat any objection as total opposition had the effect of creating several myths about Poole's opinions. Just as he turned Poole's question about sponsorship into opposition to the 1876 conference, so he turned Poole's objection to association endorsement of an unhatched scheme into opposition to the creation of a library school. In fact, Poole was more than ordinarily careful to say that he would look with interest to see the success of a library school. He did point out that the apprenticeship system had worked well in turning out good librarians, but he did not oppose the trial of a library school. What he opposed was association endorsement of the plan before it had been tried. In another connection he said:

In order that a vote of the Association, as a body, may have authority, we ought to be careful as to what we are voting upon. . . . We do too much voting. I have never asked the Association to indorse [sic] by vote any of my hobbies in methods of library work. It is enough that we have an opportunity of stating our views.[12]

Poole did not see these clashes with Dewey as major battles. He was the elder statesman, and Dewey was, to his mind, only a lightweight propagandist to be put in his place from time to time. In 1883, to be sure, Dewey overstepped the bounds when he said in a public meeting that Poole, in 1876, had invited Dewey to kick him for having opposed the conference. This assault on his dignity had to be treated seriously, and Poole reacted sharply. He wrote to Dewey that he had never made any such statement, nor had he opposed the conference once it was in proper hands. He still had in his possession letters which showed the truth of the matter, and these letters contained material which called into question Dewey's own claims to having originated the conference idea. Moreover, some of these letters were not at all complimentary to Dewey.

This sort of talk must stop, or I shall feel it necessary to say something in public which you won't like to hear. . . . I can give the public some extracts from these letters if it is necessary. I shall be very sorry to do it, but I won't be attacked by you in this way.

Concluding, Poole said:

And am I to have the statement thrown at me at every meeting of our association, when I do not go in and blow for something that you are proposing to do, and have not done, that I was an obstructionist in the formation of the Am. Library Asso., and the Library Journal? . . . Now my view of the case is that you have done me a great wrong, and owe me an apology, and a retraction.[13]

Dewey replied that he was very sorry that he had offended Poole and that, although a public statement would only draw more attention to the matter, he would promise never to repeat his remarks. Poole was mollified and, not realizing the damage the incident would do to his reputation, did not insist upon a retraction. Having set the youngster in his place, he could resume his indulgent tolerance.

In 1886 when Poole was president of the association, he gave his philosophy of librarianship in a definitive statement which, incidentally, summarized the differences between his own and Dewey's positions.

What the American librarian, in his treatment of professional topics, lacks in scholastic style, he makes up in suggestive helpful devices. He refuses to be trammelled by conventional ideas, and the solemn frown of precedent has no terror to him. He takes delight in cutting red tape; in schemes for enlarging the usefulness of his library; in contributing to the accommodation of readers; in devising shorter paths to the sources of information, and better methods in the arrangement of his books, catalogues, and indexes. All his methods and contrivances do not survive the test of experience; but some of them do. His associates have no more respect for a plan because it is *new* than because it is *old*. If it be useful it will be generally adopted. If it be not useful its ingenuity will not save it.

Going on, Poole once again expressed his belief in individuality. He described two types of librarian, each using methods which were proper because "if they have no other merit, [they] meet the conditions of his own personal equation." In this description Poole was thinking, there can be no doubt, of Dewey on the one hand, and, with little less certainty, of himself, Winsor, and perhaps his friend Lloyd P. Smith on the other.

Some librarians surround themselves with short-hand writers and much routine. Every emergency is provided for by a rule or contrivance, and every sort of business transaction, by an armory of hand-stamps. Other librarians take delight in doing work in the simplest way; in meeting emergencies as they arise; in reducing each business operation to its lowest terms, and in turning over to subordinates work which they can do well. Such librarians are not swamped in an ocean of detail; they write their own letters, are delightful correspondents, and have time to attend to the higher and bibliographical wants of their libraries.

Here Poole expressed succinctly but with color and life the essential difference between himself and Dewey. It was not, however, a veiled and pointed dig; his address was too mellow for personalities. His whole point was tolerance of diversity: "Methods which are adapted for one library are not necessarily adapted for another where conditions are different." [14]

Such tolerance was beyond the capacity of a crusader like Dewey. As the years went by, Poole found himself ever more frequently irritated by Dewey's self-righteousness and humiliated by his own membership in an association whose secretary expressed himself with such sophomoric fervor. Though the embarrassment was real, Poole could still treat it with some humor, as he did in telling Winsor that he himself did not like the "Dui" form; he preferred "Dewey" as a more accurate reflection of the young man's naïveté. [15]

Though Poole was repelled by Dewey's efforts—as one man put it—to make librarianship "one of the mechanical arts," [16] he did not take issue with Dewey's election as president in 1890. Poole was willing to grant that Dewey had earned that recognition, but when Dewey was elected to preside, in 1893, over what amounted to an international conference in Chicago, the idea of Dewey as president seemed to Poole quite grotesque. He was appalled by Dewey's pretentiousness in daring to set himself up as "the great bibliographer and librarian of the land" [17] and shocked by what he considered the steam-roller methods used by the library-school people to dominate the meeting at which Dewey was elected.

It came as a considerable blow to Poole that Dewey had come to wield so much power, but, even if he had foreseen this development, it is doubtful that he would have mounted an offensive to cut Dewey's influence. Before the end of his career he was thoroughly annoyed with Dewey, and he disliked both Dewey's mechanical devices and his classification system, which he viewed as just one more rigid mechanism. But these were the personal privileges of each individual, and the whole point all through their rivalry, so far as Poole was concerned, was that each librarian should be allowed to pursue his own course. Dewey, the crusader, had been fighting throughout the years against all who opposed his ideas; Poole had asked only to be allowed to express his opinions and to do as he thought best. The battle which was fought from 1876 to 1894 was one in which only Dewey was seriously engaged.

The contest was never one which occupied Poole's attention except in moments of irritation. It was far from the keynote of his participation in the association. Over the years he attended the meetings for the personal satisfaction of renewing warm friendships and for the professional stimulation he received from the part he took in the meetings. The association gave him an opportunity to participate in the growth of librarianship on a broader stage than was afforded him in his day-to-day work in Chicago. And, more important in his contribution to librarianship, it provided organizational backing for the completion and publication of a new edition of the *Index*.

VIII. Poole's Index

The American Library Association was an important factor in the preparation of the great third edition of the *Index*. The early editions of 1848 and 1853 had been pioneering ventures. Had no later edition been published, they would have been interesting historical relics, and the second edition might have retained some value as a guide to the contents of the periodicals of the time. The publication of the third edition set in motion the work that, with its successor volumes, forms an unbroken series and continues to make Poole's name a byword among initiated scholars.

During the years following 1853, Poole kept up his interest in preparing a new edition, and, on at least two occasions, there were hints that it was well on the way to completion. So far as the record shows, however, the work had lain dormant since 1870 when Joseph Henry refused support for publication from Smithsonian Institution funds. At the 1876 conference of librarians, it was inevitable that the question of a new edition would arise, and, indeed, so great was the interest of the librarians present that they refused to wait until the time designated in the program to discuss it. As soon as indexing was mentioned in another connection, they rose, one after another, to attest to the great value of the 1853 edition and to the cost and labor required to keep the indexing of periodicals up to date. There were suggestions that one person be employed to do the job for all libraries; Poole proposed a different plan. He suggested that all the libraries represented there, augmented by others, agree to divide the many periodicals among them, that the indexing be done locally in each of these institutions under a set of rules to be established, and that the entries be sent to a central bureau for editing and revising. He himself would operate the bureau, with such help as he needed. The work which he had already done he would contribute to the cause. After completion of the main volume, supplements would be issued at intervals of five years, or more frequently if necessary. It was moved that the matter be referred to a supervisory committee for action. After further testimonial and comment, the motion, with Poole himself in the chair, was passed unanimously. With that, work on the monumental third edition of *Poole's Index* was officially launched.

Immediately after the Philadelphia meeting, Poole went on eastward, stopping in Hartford to enlist his old friend of Athenaeum and Waterbury days, William I. Fletcher, as his principal associate in the project. In Boston he met with Winsor and Cutter, who were the other members of the committee on cooperative indexing appointed in Philadelphia. That meeting produced agreement that the new edition was to continue on the same basis as the old, being a subject and not an author index. The committee would prepare a set of rules and a list of periodicals to be assigned to the participating libraries. The periodicals would be limited to those in English of general and literary interest. Scientific and professional journals would not be included as a rule, although references might be made to articles of lay interest in a few leading scientific periodicals.

During the next months work went forward on preparing the list and formulating the rules. These rules contained certain specific instructions but left a great deal to the judgment of the individual indexer. Poole's touch was most distinctively present in the general admonition:

The indexer will find a resolution of many of his doubts if he keeps constantly in mind the main object of his work, which is to show as completely and accurately as possible the real subjects treated, rather than to make a technical index to any particular series. References to trivial and inconsequential matters must be avoided.[1]

Pragmatic and optimistic, Poole never got over his possibly naive assumption that people are intelligent and can be trusted to use good judgment.

The detailed procedural instructions are interesting, since they undoubtedly describe the methods Poole himself had used during those countless nights of his lifetime when he sat indexing the volumes he carried home on the train in the evening and returned to the library the next morning. The indexer was to use sheets of lined paper. Taking a single volume, he should turn to the first article, writing on the first line of the paper the abridged title, inverted to bring out the subject as the first word, and then the author's name in parentheses, the abbreviation for the periodical title, the volume number, followed by a colon, and the number of the first page of the article. On the second line he should give, if necessary, a second entry to bring out another aspect of the subject content. On this line and on succeeding lines on the page, he should omit the name of the periodical, remembering, however, to repeat it on the first line of each page. These names could be filled in later more easily and more accurately, with a rubber stamp if possible, than if done by the indexer as he went along. To guard against loss, each sheet should be numbered before being sent to the central bureau. Alphabetical arrangement of the entries could be ignored by the indexer, since the entries would be cut apart and arranged later.

In the discussions of the rules and procedures, other librarians made themselves heard. The discussions centered around three important questions: the choice of entry, the method of doing the work, and the source of financial support.

Walter S. Biscoe, one of Dewey's close associates, wrote an article for the April, 1877, issue of the *Library Journal*, in which, after the customary genuflection to Poole's 1853 volume, he criticized it for its adherence to the word choice of the authors themselves. He pointed out that Poole's plan resulted in scattered references to articles on the same subject as a consequence of the use of many different synonyms. References appeared, he said, under such similar entries as Cemeteries, Churchyards, and Graveyards. As a solution, he proposed the establishment of a list of headings agreed upon in advance. He preferred a classified arrangement of the headings but conceded that this question might well be the subject of further discussion. In 1878, when an editorial suggestion appeared in the *Library Journal* contending that a classified arrangement should be used, Poole firmly rejected it:

The fatal defect of every classified arrangement is that nobody understands it except the person who made it, and he is often in doubt, while an alphabetical arrangement is so simple that the stupidest mortal can understand it without explanation.[2]

In the same way, the suggestion for the use of a standard list of headings was rejected, since, according to the rules committee, the title given by the author was usually the best expression of the subject of the article. The promise of the abundant use of cross references did not really answer Biscoe's objection. His proposal aimed at reducing the dispersal of entries on the same subject; the promised cross references would only help the reader to find all the scattered entries. With Poole in control, strongly backed by Winsor and Cutter, the basic plan of the *Index* was not to be changed lightly.

At the 1877 meeting of the association, a group tried once again to press the suggestion that the work be done by one person employed for the purpose by the various libraries, using a "combination of capital" rather than a "combination of labor." [3] Winsor made adroit use of his prestige and position to head off any considerable debate in this effort to change the plan of operation.

The question of money arose again at the meeting in connection with an apprehension that the association might be financially committed. Poole promptly rose to say: "I never have understood that the Association had any responsibility in this matter. . . . If the thing does not pay, I am willing to stand all pecuniary responsibility." [4] Even so, enough members felt uneasy that a resolution was passed specifically disclaiming financial obligation.

Poole's firm rejection of efforts to change the plan of procedure and the clear exclusion of the association from fiscal responsibility—and therefore authority—were important factors in the ultimate success of the cooperative venture. The participating librarians were given an opportunity to be heard, but final decisions and ultimate responsibility were left, in part, to Poole, Winsor, and Cutter in their capacity as the committee and, in part, to Poole alone. As time passed, it became clear that both Winsor and Cutter were inclined to defer to Poole. One reason the arduous task could be completed was that, however many voices might be heard in advice and debate, the authority and responsibility lay with a single individual.

Later, when Poole had finished the work, he expressed his views on the essential requirements of such a cooperative venture. He believed that one of the most important results of his work was the demonstration that such achievements were possible using cooperative means. He was equally positive that the direction must be in the hands of one individual. "Committees can do some things admirably . . . but they cannot conduct a campaign, or do anything which requires administrative ability and executive oversight. One mind must have full charge of the enterprise." This man, he said, should be one "who will command the confidence of the profession, who will put his own individuality in the work, and conduct it with something of autocratic sway." [5] In regard to a similar project then being proposed, he estimated that the work could be done within six months so long as the work was to represent "simply the judgment of the chief editor. If the list were submitted to a committee, and they were expected to agree, my estimate would be widely erroneous. A position on that committee would not be an enviable one, and might prove to be a life estate." [6]

Although the enterprise was under Poole's "autocratic sway," it was still a cooperative venture and took time to get started. By February, 1878, enough libraries had reported their holdings that he was able to assign more than a hundred titles to participating libraries. The difficulties came, not from a want of volunteers, but from the willingness of so many librarians from small institutions to participate. Since the periodicals in the small collections tended to duplicate one another, Poole was hard-pressed to find work for all of them. He withheld assignments from some of the large libraries in order to allot as many titles as possible to smaller institutions. Now he was ready to begin to "punch up the libraries that had not responded." [7] It was not serious if small libraries chose not to participate, but the large ones must join if all the desired periodicals were to be included. Thus, Poole wrote to N. H. Morison, provost of the Peabody Institute of Baltimore, seeking cooperation and, having secured his agreement, assigned scientific journals to whose indexing the librarian, P. R. Uhler, could bring his special knowledge. In general, Poole tried to get specialists to index periodicals in their own fields. He assigned the *New England Historical and Genealogical Register* to Edmund M. Barton of the American Antiquarian Society, for, he said:

It is work which should be done by a person like yourself skilled in New England history, and knowing the relative value of historical articles. We do not intend to index everything in a periodical but only such articles as have sufficient importance to have a place in such a general Index. Hence knowledge and good judgment is needed, and I was about to say also "a good deal of the grace of God" in doing such work. I have always found it more difficult to decide what to *leave* out than what to *include*.[8]

Yale must take its share too, not only because it had a large library, but because Poole had "a pride that Yale should gallantly help out the Committee, as here was where the Index started." He thought Addison Van Name, the librarian, would be able to enlist the assistance of "some zealous student who will be glad to help you on this work, and who will work with the same motive that inspired me when I made my first and second edition of the Index." [9]

The task was going well. By the end of March Poole had made assignments to most of the libraries and was ready to allot the remaining titles to the four large institutions, the Boston Public, the Athenaeum, the Astor, and the Library of Congress, which he had purposely left to the last. During the assignment process, Poole met little resistance or unwillingness. Indeed, he said: "I am greatly pleased that the great libraries have gone into this work so zealously. They take just what I allot to them without a bit of grumbling, but, on the other hand, as if they liked it." [10]

In giving substantial assignments to others, Poole was by no means shirking the task himself. He wrote, he said, twenty letters a day relating to the *Index*. In addition, he was at work on the indexing himself. "I have indexed more than 100 volumes the past month, and I can keep it up at this rate. I work till midnight regularly, and find it does not disagree with me." [11] Later, describing his work on more than 600 volumes, he said: "I indexed every one of them myself in my own home twelve miles from the city after 9 o'clock at night. I carried these vols out in my hands and returned them in the same way to the library." [12]

Before April, 1878, all allotments had been made except for twelve titles reserved for British librarians and four not reported by any library. The contributors were to be allowed six months to complete their part of the work. The assignments to British libraries took longer than those to American institutions, partly because Robert Harrison of the London Library, though chairman of the committee, had, as he confessed, little faith in the cooperative principle as a way of accomplishing such work. Perhaps one fundamental reason for the British reluctance was the fact that the enterprise was not really their own. Finally, in June, a circular was published by the British committee seeking volunteers among their colleagues, and twenty-four titles were taken by twenty British librarians. With widespread cooperation promised and assignments made, it was hoped that most of the raw data would be in the hands of the central bureau sometime during the fall.

For the next few years, the *Index* occupied the center of Poole's attention. He was busy as well with other things, but there was, until the middle of 1880, a notable absence of activities which were not concerned with the *Index,* the Chicago library, or a few other enterprises to which his participation was already committed. Throughout his life, Poole tended to be dissatisfied with only one or two activities. He might concentrate for a time on a few projects if they were unusually pressing, but, as soon as he had one thing finished, he embarked on another. During the period from the spring of 1878 until the middle of 1880, Poole worked on the *Index* to the exclusion of everything else, except those activities to which he already owed an obligation.

Periodically, discussion appeared in the *Library Journal* as various librarians still sought to debate the details of the plan for the *Index,* and a number of people wrote to Poole asking how the work was going. He finally made a public apology for his failure to reply to inquiries, for to do so, he said, would leave little time to work on the *Index.* When he was finally driven to reply to the critics of his plan, he asked to be spared further argument:

If the enterprise were delayed until these details were settled on a basis which satisfied everybody, we should look in vain for the publication in this century. . . .

An immense burden of labor and responsibility has been laid upon the editors of the new Index. The confidence and sympathy of the collaborators and of the library profession will lighten this burden. The editors have time to be instructed and encouraged, but have no time for controversy.[13]

Controversy or not, the work took longer than the six months from April, 1878, originally suggested, but it is doubtful that Poole ever thought of this deadline as more than a moving target. When, in the middle of 1879, he reported that five sixths of the contributions had been received, he asked all participants to send in references to periodicals for 1879, work which could not be completed until the next year. April 1, 1880, was finally set as the last date for the receipt of contributions.

Even after the entries were received, there was a great deal of editing to do. Not until February of 1881 did Poole complete 600 manuscript pages of copy for the printer. In July, page 2,106 marked what he estimated to be half the work. Finally, on January 16, 1882, he reported: "I have on my desk the last sheet of my 'Index to Period. Lit.' " [14] Without asking further help from contributors, he and Fletcher indexed the 1880 and 1881 volumes of all periodicals. The work went off to the publisher, James R. Osgood and Company. From April until late in the year, he and Fletcher had to read more than 1,400 pages of proof, but Poole was not dismayed. "The work will go on like mice," he said.[15] In November all proof had been corrected, and Poole sent off the manuscript for the preface. Before the end of December the book was published.

A royal octavo of 27 prefatory and 1,442 main pages, the new *Index* was a large and handsome book. With double columns on each page, it contained some 230,000 entries covering 6,205 volumes of 232 different periodicals. The work was priced at $15.00 in cloth, $17.00 in sheep, and $18.00 in half morocco.

The reviewers, without exception, praised the volume. It was a tremendous achievement whose merits were obvious to all. The *Library Journal* did not attempt to evaluate it: "To librarians it is not necessary to praise this book, and to criticize would require months of use. Its faults, if it has any, are not on the surface." A representative of the scientists, who might have been expected to complain of the omission of technical journals, was, on the contrary, generous in praise, not just of the literary material indexed but also of the quantity of scientific references as well, saying that it supplied an important need for a way to find articles on "the personality of scientific men." Far from being scornful of the popular science articles included, the reviewer pointed to the "solid and permanent value" of such material. "Whatever a truly competent investigator has to say is likely to be worth hearing; and even his colleagues may gain a clearer conception of his thought by listening to his attempts at popular simplification." [16]

Others mixed criticism with their praise. One, indeed, questioned whether it was worth "the enormous labour it must have cost" and wondered whether "its necessarily enormous size and the unavoidable technicalities of method and arrangement will not tend largely to detract from such popularity as it might otherwise attain." [17] Another suggested that reprint journals, like *Littell's Living Age,* might well have been omitted, since most of the material was covered by references to the original articles. In fact, of course, such citations were particularly useful in American libraries that did not have the English journals from which most of these articles were reprinted. The rest of the criticism repeated the same old arguments against the failure to use a standard list of subject headings or a classified arrangement of entries.

The reviewers' criticisms were all balanced by generous praise. Even the *Nation,* whose review Poole evidently considered unfavorable, ended its list of objections with the statement that "these are slight blemishes in a great and useful work." The *Athenaeum* said: "Mr. Poole may well be proud of a work which will make his name famous on both sides of the Atlantic, and Chicago may well be proud of the industry and energy of her librarian." The *Academy* reviewer said: "Certainly one of the greatest and most practical of Transatlantic bibliographers is Dr. Poole, whom we have now to congratulate on the completion of a work that will earn him the gratitude of scholars alike in the Old World and in the New." [18]

This use of the term "Dr. Poole" was the result of an honor that must have pleased him. The Poole family had moved to Evanston in 1880, and, in June of 1882, Northwestern University conferred on its local citizen the LL.D. degree in recognition of his contributions to scholarship in his library work and in the preparation of the *Index.*

The honor of the degree and the praise of the reviewers were pleasant to receive. They had been earned at the cost of a great deal of labor, which left Poole, for a brief time, too tired for any of the writing he customarily did in his spare moments. "I had a sort of intellectual lassitude which shunned work. The pressure had been on me so long and so persistently that poor human nature demanded a rest." [19] But only a month after the volume was published, he reported that he was ready to begin his outside activities once again. Until the time came to work intensively on the *Index* supplement, he could return to the historical writing that occupied many of his evening hours.

Poole's writing during his Chicago years consisted largely of book reviews published in the local newspapers and, after 1881, in *The Dial*. Almost invariably, the books he considered were historical works, and his review of Theodore Roosevelt's *The Winning of the West,* published in the *Atlantic Monthly,* led to a mutually admiring exchange of correspondence with the future President.

In addition to many book reviews, Poole wrote a chapter for each of two cooperative histories that Winsor edited. In "Witchcraft in Boston," for the *Memorial History of Boston,* he returned to his old interest in Cotton Mather's part in the Salem trials. For the *Narrative and Critical History of America,* Poole covered the Western campaigns during the twenty years up to the end of the Revolutionary War. One of his most substantial efforts, it was also one of his least able. Although it was evidently based on extensive research, the chapter was too much a recitation of successive episodes and too little a cohesive whole. In 1888, when Poole was president of the American Historical Association, his address was entitled "The Early Northwest." Essentially a reworking of earlier writings, it was oriented toward pointing out the richness of Western history and the abundance of opportunity for work in new and important historical problems. Although based on considerable command of his subject matter and expressed with his usual force and color, Poole's writings during his years in Chicago lacked the originality and interpretative power of some of his earlier articles. The hours after nine at night were not sufficient to allow him to develop fully his capacity for striking new historical studies. It is evident that his life as a librarian and an indexer took a large part of his time.

In 1883 Poole presented to the American Library Association conference a plan to issue annual supplements which would then be cumulated to form the promised five-year supplements. The annual issues would not be likely to have a sale sufficient to justify a publisher's taking the risk of a regular trade publication. Thus, sale would be by advance subscription only, with no one receiving any compensation except that the contributors would be given a free copy and the editors would be allowed to use the material for the cumulations. In the meantime, Fletcher had begun a series of monthly—soon changed to quarterly—indexes, printed as supplements to the *Library Journal*. This material too would go into the annual volume. The periodicals to be included totaled 103 titles to be distributed among thirty-four contributors. Poole had not found it difficult to get volunteers. Indeed, he said, the big problem had been to find enough work for all who wanted to help. Anyone else who wished to join would have to bring with him the title of a new periodical. Poole himself apologized for seeming to be "greedy" in taking so many for himself. "I must confess that I like this sort of work." [20]

Although Poole had enjoyed the praise of the *Index* in reviews and in personal correspondence, the Buffalo conference of 1883 gave him his first opportunity to receive in person the congratulations of most of his colleagues. Winsor, in his presidential address, named the completion of the *Index* as the most notable of the year's accomplishments, a reference which brought applause from the delegates. Just as Poole had said in the preface to his work, Winsor maintained that even more important than the published volume was the evidence it offered that cooperation could produce many useful works needed by libraries.

The high hopes for the success of cooperation were not realized in the annual issues. When, in April, 1884, Poole and Fletcher reported that the manuscript was complete and sought subscriptions, the response did not reach 300, the minimum number required to allow copies to be supplied at even the high price of $6.50. This result was taken to mean that the annual volume could not be sustained. The manuscript was kept to be used in the five-year supplement and was regularly augmented, but, even more than he had expected, Poole was freed from responsibility for the *Index*.

All during these years, however, Poole kept a keen interest in the progress of sales of the 1882 volume. The book had been published with a subsidy, in that Poole himself had paid more than $6,000 for the plates. It was probably for this purpose that he borrowed $3,000 in October, 1882, taking out a mortgage on the house in Melrose. Presumably, Osgood had paid for paper, press-run, binding, and other costs. It was also the publisher's responsibility to advertise and sell the book. In Poole's view, Osgood had made a good profit on orders which came in almost automatically. Rather than pay for promotion and advertising, Poole thought, Osgood preferred to sit back and take the profits which came to him from a moderate sale. Only if the book were pushed vigorously could Poole hope to get his own money back. In the summer of 1884 he offered to buy the rights and all unsold copies at cost in order that he might be free to promote the sale himself. He was not a complete stranger to book publishing, having issued, from plates which he owned, an edition of Jared Sparks's *Works of Benjamin Franklin*. The Osgood firm did not accept Poole's offer but promised to push the book more vigorously, a pledge that Poole felt was not honored. Then, in the spring of 1885, James R. Osgood and Company fell into financial difficulty and suspended operation. When Benjamin Holt Ticknor took over the company, he proposed to renew the contract, promising vigorous promotion. Poole again offered to buy the rights and stock, but again the publishing house kept its control. Poole believed that he himself could have sold more copies. He said that more than a hundred copies had been bought by individuals in Chicago alone. The large libraries had bought duplicate copies for their use, but, in all, not many more than a thousand had been sold by September, 1885. Poole said that he saw, at the moment, no hope of getting back the money he had invested. "There is something left, however, in the locker for the publication of the five-year supplements." [21] In saying this, he may have been thinking of money left from the $5,000 he received free and clear from sale of the Melrose house in 1884. Despite his experience with every edition, including the proposed annual supplements, he remained optimistic that such a work, properly promoted, could pay for itself. Early in 1886 Poole had the opportunity to try his hand at selling when the Ticknor firm finally let him take over the rights. Whether it was the result of his efforts or not, he had received enough return by 1887 to reduce his investment to $3,000. The financial outcome of the *Index,* so far as Poole was concerned, is lost with his personal accounts. It is likely, however, that he eventually got his money back and perhaps even began to profit. By 1891, the 1882 edition being out of print, he assigned the publication rights to Houghton, Mifflin and Company and corrected the errors in preparation for a revised edition, which was published in 1893.

Poole continued to bear financial and editorial responsibility for the *Index* and, for the 1887 supplement, he also did a good deal of work. He himself indexed 73 periodicals representing 435 volumes, almost exactly 40 percent of the 1,089 volumes indexed. The work of indexing, however, was the mere preliminary to the preparation of the supplement, and Poole gave credit for most of the editorial work to Fletcher. About half the material in the supplement had been printed before, under Fletcher's sole editorship, for his *Cooperative Index to Current Periodicals.* This portion required only general review before its entries were arranged with the new material sent in by the fifty-nine contributors. All that may be said unequivocally of Poole's part in the volume is that he signed the preface and that he was listed as making by far the largest single contribution. The preface has the ring of Poole's language, though Fletcher also signed it. Poole may have read the proof, but it seems less likely that he helped to assemble the copy for the printers. Printing began soon after the beginning of 1888 and was largely finished by July. Late in September, 1888, the volume finally appeared.

This supplement was still *Poole's Index* in its title, but it was no longer his in the way that the first three versions had been. And it ended his participation in the production of the work. In one sense, he was the living embodiment of *Poole's Index*—the *Library Journal* suggested that the dictionary should define "Poole" as "a catalogue of periodical literature" [22]—but, for several years, he had steadily become less closely connected with it.

Fletcher continued the work, bringing out a second supplement in 1893. In 1897 the third supplement was published, with Fletcher being assisted by Poole's nephew, Franklin Osborn Poole, who was later well known as librarian of the Association of the Bar of New York. In the work of the fourth supplement (1903) and the fifth (1908), Fletcher collaborated with Poole's daughter Mary. These two also brought out in 1901 an abridged edition, covering thirty-seven periodicals and adapted for small libraries, and a supplement to it in 1905. As early as 1904 Fletcher felt the competition of the H. W. Wilson Company's *Readers' Guide to Periodical Literature* and published a defensive statement pointing out the advantages of *Poole's Index* in coverage and comprehensiveness. The frequently cumulated Wilson index drove *Poole's Index* from the field; it could not survive against the principle of Jewett's *"mud catalogue."* So far as Poole himself was concerned, the *Index* played little part in his life after 1887. His outside activities centered around the American Library Association and, for a time, the American Historical Association. From then on, he was able to devote his evenings to his various studies and writings. His daily work, as always, was devoted to his own library in Chicago.

IX. Later Years at the
Chicago Public Library, 1879-1886

Poole's participation in the American Library Association and his editorial work on the *Index* accompanied but never replaced his day-to-day responsibilities in the Chicago Public Library. The promising beginning of 1874 was followed by a long period when funds were scarce and services barely sustained. Finally, for the year 1879–80, a substantial increase in the budget was granted. Even so, it took some time for the library to recover and to rebuild its collection and services. The next year a further increase allowed the restoration of the salary cuts made during the lean years. From that time on the library's funds were usually increased each year. During the next seven years the Library began to realize some of its early promise.

With money again available, the collection began to grow once more. Whereas only 2,000 volumes had been added in 1878–79, the next year brought an increase of 8,000, and the year after that 12,000. Between 1882 and 1886, although accessions varied somewhat, they were always substantial, averaging 10,000 volumes per year. In a period of seven years, up to the middle of 1886, the library doubled its collection to a total of 120,000 volumes.

As the book collection grew, the use of the library increased. Although the depletion resulting from the lack of funds was finally reflected in a drop of circulation to only about 300,000 loans during 1879–80, the recovery was steady after that time. By 1883–84 circulation climbed well above 400,000, increasing by another 100,000 the next year, and by 1885–86 it was over 600,000.

One reason for the rise in circulation was the inauguration of a new service in June, 1884. As the city grew and the residential districts extended farther and farther from the center, it became apparent that the library must make its services available to people near their homes. Chicago could not afford to establish full-fledged branch libraries as Boston had done more than a decade before, but, as an intermediate step, six delivery stations were established during 1884. These delivery stations were not, in any real sense, branch libraries. They were simply retail stores whose proprietors had agreed to receive orders for books. The orders were given to a messenger who came twice a day to receive them, to deliver books to the store proprietor to hold until the patrons called for them, and to return both books and further orders to the library. The storekeepers were at first paid a small fee for their work. It was soon found that the delivery stations brought so many people into the stores that the increase in business more than repaid the proprietors for the trouble of operating these distribution centers. Eventually, the storekeepers were no longer paid, and the only cost to the library was the sum required for the pick-up and delivery of books.

The delivery stations proved to be a complete success. They were so popular that citizens in other neighborhoods petitioned for establishment of similar outlets, requests which the library found embarrassing because it could not afford the expense of many additions to the system. Poole suggested that perhaps the library had fulfilled its responsibility once it had made its books available at a central location and that it might be justified in making a charge for delivery of books to the stations. This suggestion was not adopted, but, despite the extra costs, eight delivery stations were in operation before Poole left the Chicago Public Library in 1887. The success of one of the last stations to be established illustrates the way in which the new service enabled the library to reach those who had never come to the central collection. Located in a neighborhood where immigrants from Bohemia predominated, it soon became the most popular of the stations, and the dramatic rise in the use of books in the Bohemian language demonstrated that it was serving people who had never before used the library. In this instance, as in the case of other language groups, the library did not hesitate to buy popular works in foreign languages to meet the demands of immigrant groups. In 1880–81, for example, foreign-language books comprised almost one fifth of the collection, with French, German, and the Scandinavian languages predominating.

The delivery stations took the library's services to the people where they lived but did not replace the main collections. Poole had said in 1874 that, regardless of what outlets might be established in remote parts of the city, "the Central Library will always be the main resort of scholars, and those interested in the higher departments of literature." [1] In the years after that time, a formal department to serve this group was developed in the library. At first the reference books had been kept on open shelves in the reading room. As a result of a move to new quarters in the middle of 1875 and in response to a number of thefts, these books were moved into a protected space equipped with its own tables and chairs. From that beginning a reference department began to grow. The early gifts after the Fire, being often the formal donations from governments and other official bodies, tended to be the sort of books more suitable for reference than for popular reading. Most notable of these was a set of patent reports given by the British government. Poole solicited other such gifts over the years from state governments, from the federal government, and from learned societies. By 1876 he was speaking explicitly in terms of a reference department and arranged that users of that department could call for more than one book at a time, the limit allowed to other patrons. Although crowded quarters prevented the full flowering of the department before 1886, it gained in popularity and use so steadily that, despite the constantly increasing need for more space all over the library, additional tables were set up for this function year by year. In 1882 the growing importance of the reference collection as contrasted with the lending collection in the main building was reflected in a change by which the circulation department closed at 8:30 P.M., half an hour earlier than before, while the reference department and reading room remained open an hour longer than previously, until 10 P.M. Poole himself considered that reference assistance was his own particular responsibility, regularly emphasizing that "my office door is always open, and anybody seeking for information is encouraged to come to me directly and without formality." [2] Although the effect of the hospitably open door may have been somewhat lessened by the placard "Be Short" which he placed over it, perhaps the geniality of his greeting took any sting from the sign. One of his assistants recalled Poole's cordiality:

His friends were warm friends, and he loved them dearly. He was never too tired nor too busy to greet them. I remember particularly, his habit of taking their hand in both of his—while his handsome brown eyes would gleam and his face light up with a benignant smile.[3]

To unknown inquirers he might not have been so effusive, but he must have made welcome those who sought the assistance which he called "one of the most pleasant duties of my position." [4]

Assistance to readers in the reference department was only one of the ways Poole encouraged users of the library. He had never followed the practice of restricting service to patrons on the basis of age, believing that fostering reading among the young was one of the most important duties of the library. This service, however, was not performed by a separate department. Poole heartily approved of the work being done at the Hartford Library Association by Caroline M. Hewins, whom he had trained at the Athenaeum, but even that pioneer in service to young people had not yet progressed so far as to establish a formal children's department. The Chicago library, through its separate circulation file for juvenile borrowers, did arrange a situation in which specific attendants could become especially acquainted with the juvenile collection and with some of its regular borrowers, but separate, planned service to children by specialists had yet to come to American libraries.

Poole believed that much of the assistance and guidance to children in their reading should be done through the schools. To encourage this work, he launched in 1882 a project to bring the library into a close relationship with the schools. In March of that year he addressed the principals of the schools, urging the accomplishment of three objectives: the teachers should be led to undertake the guidance of children's reading, the library should be brought into close touch with school children, and the students should be taught how to use the library for independent study. Following that meeting, the principals compiled a list of books suitable for children, and some of them took the initiative to raise money for books to begin school libraries. Although these efforts had Poole's hearty endorsement, he continued to try to bring the school children into the library. "Instructing students in the elements of bibliography, methods of study, etc.," in his view, was "the work above all others for librarians now to give their attention to." [5] For that purpose, he led the Chicago library to institute—as many other libraries were doing—a new program of service to schools.

Beginning in January, 1883, and continuing for seventeen weeks, classes numbering about fifty students were brought to the library on Saturday mornings to attend a lecture conducted by their teacher and by Poole himself. He usually opened the meeting by emphasizing the importance of independent study, telling the pupils that they were learning in school only the tools of study and that their real education would begin with their own studies after they left school. The difference between the educated and the uneducated, he said, was not so much a difference in amount of information as a difference in knowledge of the means to acquire information. For that purpose, books were the tools of the educated man in the same way that pliers, hammers, and screwdrivers were the tools of the skilled mechanic. "Few books can be read consecutively; but all books may be used as works of reference, and that is their highest purpose." [6] He then displayed and demonstrated the use of reference books which had been brought in especially for the meeting. Concluding with an invitation to the students to use the library freely and to consult him when they needed help, he turned over the meeting to the teacher, who spoke on a special subject of the day. Following the meeting, the class was taken on a tour of the library, and the pupils were given application forms for borrowers' cards. As a supplement to this program of lectures, it was arranged that the principals (later individual teachers were given the same privilege) could borrow groups of books to be used in the schools and loaned to the students from the classrooms.

In its formal aspects, this program of service to the schools did not continue for very long. The next year twenty-seven lectures were delivered, the following year only seven, and the year after that none. Poole was disappointed that the principals and teachers did not take their responsibilities for guiding their pupils' reading as seriously as he thought they should, but he continued to speak hopefully of closer cooperation between the library and the schools in the future. In fact, the venture had one result which helped to make the program less necessary. The experience of having books in the classrooms encouraged a number of schools to collect libraries of their own. By 1885 twenty-three of the schools had a total of 11,000 volumes among them.

His work with the schools and his assistance to individual readers were manifestations of a new enthusiasm in Poole's life. He now began to place new emphasis on the educational mission of the public library. This idea was not new to him; a main purpose stressed in his advocacy of fiction had been that novels would eventually lead the reader to better reading. Clearly, even as long before as the first edition of his *Index,* he had been interested in assistance to readers, but now the emphasis on education became much greater. He supplied the rationale for his position at a meeting of the American Library Association in 1883:

Our Public Libraries and our Public Schools are supported by the same constituencies, by the same methods of taxation, and for the same purpose; and that purpose is the education of the people. For no other object would a general tax for the support of public libraries be justifiable. If public libraries shall, in my day, cease to be educational institutions, and serve only to amuse the people and help them to while away an idle hour, I shall favor their abolition.[7]

Here Poole was retreating from his previous view that, in a democracy, any service was warranted if demanded by a majority of the people, even the provision of novels for reading purely as a pastime. He did not mean, however, to abandon fiction. The Chicago Public Library continued to carry novels in its collections. As late as 1892 Poole was still advocating the view that children at least—and probably he meant uneducated adults as well—must be allowed wide latitude in selecting reading which appealed to them. And he kept his faith that, given freedom, they would soon improve in taste. When challenged on that point, he was fond of telling about his experience with a city councilman's wife whose social position had risen above the level of her cultural background. In despair because she could not understand the literary works recommended by her friends as a means of self-improvement, she turned to Poole. He started her with the novels of Mary

Jane Holmes and gradually led her through those of Augusta Evans and Mrs. Southworth to the substantial fiction of Dickens, Scott, Thackeray, and Eliot. She became, he said, a serious and accomplished reader. He continued to believe that even light and sentimental fiction had a proper place in a public library, but he no longer maintained that it was justified on the grounds of its value as a pastime. They were, he said, necessary first steps toward better reading.

Although Poole might speak rhetorically of the abolition of public libraries, his passion continued to be their establishment. Ever since he had moved to Cincinnati, he had been consulted regularly by those seeking advice on the best methods to follow. When, in 1880, he moved his home to Evanston, he began immediately to take an interest in its public library. The first summer he wrote for the local paper an article which may well represent his customary approach to encouraging the establishment and development of such institutions. Characteristically, he appealed to the practical sense and civic pride of the citizens, maintaining that public libraries, like gas, running water, bathrooms, and window screens, were a "modern improvement" which every forward-looking community must consider a necessity of life. He not only pointed to the great values to be conferred on the citizens of a community by a library, but he went so far as to maintain that it was an investment whose cost would be returned in the form of increased land values. He urged that citizens supplement the regular municipal appropriation by a general subscription drive to buy books to give the library the kind of collection it should have.[8]

Encouragement to other libraries was only a minor duty of Chicago's librarian. His principal responsibility was supervision of all activities of the library and close personal attention to some of them. Although W. B. Wickersham, as secretary, was responsible directly to the board for the accounts and for securing supplies and equipment, he was, as assistant librarian, Poole's chief representative in supervising the attendants. When disciplinary problems arose, however, Poole himself took care of them. One of Poole's most important assignments was to select the books to be purchased. For that purpose, he read 1,000 to 1,500 pages of dealers' catalogs each week, much of it at night. With a collection approaching 100,000 volumes, selection proved an exacting task. He kept the statistics of circulation. He represented the library in person in his work with the school children, in meetings with civic groups, and even, on occasion, with Congressional committees. He maintained a large official correspondence. In his own office he closely directed two assistants who ordered books, arranged pamphlets, kept track of serial publications and claimed issues not received, arranged public documents, and kept such records of the collection as the card catalog, the accession book, the shelf lists, and copy for the finding lists. All of these duties, Poole boasted, were performed by three people, whereas the Boston Public Library, although it acquired only a few more books each year, employed twenty-one for the purpose.

The work with the card catalog and the finding lists represented practices which differed from those of many other libraries. Poole was not persuaded that the card catalog could safely be made available to the public without the mediation of an attendant. As a substitute in the library and as a means of providing the patrons with a record they could take home, the printed finding lists continued to be kept up to date by periodic new editions and interim supplements. They were an essential part of the system of delivery stations, for without them the patrons would have had no way of knowing what books were available. The ingenuity of the printer who saw an opportunity to make a profit through the sale of advertisements had brought the price of the lists down to a low figure and had relieved the library of all printing costs. When Poole began in the early years to make these lists, he had considered them a useful but inadequate substitute for a printed catalog. After eleven years of experience, he was ready to claim for his innovation an important place in library administration:

The Finding List seems to fully meet the demands of the public for a printed inventory of the books, and it practically answers one of the most controverted and difficult questions which has arisen in the administration of rapidly-growing libraries with large constituencies of book-borrowers: "How can readers best be served with late and frequently-revised lists of books contained in the library?" [9]

The introduction of new services and the growth of old ones were accompanied by some problems. A minor difficulty was a fear which arose in 1879 that library books might be the means of spreading disease. Poole doubted that there was any real danger, but he thought the anxiety too important to ignore. Letters were written asking opinions from leading medical authorities and librarians. The conclusion, given wide publicity in Chicago, was that, while theoretically possible, the chances of the actual spread of disease were very slight, similar, as Poole put it, to the likelihood that "a person may be struck by lightning in February, but I never heard of such a case and do not worry about it." [10] Still, just on the chance, the Health Commissioner was asked to notify the library of homes with contagious diseases so that library books in them could be fumigated before being put back in circulation. Poole was well satisfied with the action taken. "My plan of going to the bottom of this thing, and not dodging the issue I think has been the best way of treating it. The demon is laid." [11]

The policy of frank disclosure also served Poole well in connection with a series of thefts from the collections. Minor pilferage was always a problem, but in 1884 the annual inventory disclosed the absence of a disturbingly large number of books. Poole did not attempt to minimize the problem. Although he did not think it wise to establish a rigid system of surveillance, he relieved the attendant of certain distracting duties and rearranged the furniture to provide improved oversight of the books in the reference department. At the same time, he invited the board to consider the problem and to suggest any changes it thought wise. Meanwhile, he met privately with some of the board members, and with their help began a quiet investigation. Ultimately, suspicion settled on an evening attendant in the reading room. When the police searched the man's room, about a hundred books were found. Publicity given to the case led to a further discovery when a policeman in an outlying district reported that he had seen the attendant carrying books into a nearby barn. A further search turned up a total of more than two thousand books which the attendant had taken. The astounding dimensions of the theft shook both Poole and the board. They had acted wisely throughout the difficulty, however: first, in not becoming so panicky that they instituted inquisitorial methods of control; second, in their frank admission of the difficulties; and, third, in their quiet and persistent investigation which

Poole in His Office at the Chicago Public Library

eventually solved the mystery. It was found that the culprit had a previous record of book thefts which he had concealed by a change of name and by a new career as a well-regarded student at the University of Chicago. The fact that he had been employed on the strength of recommendations from the president of the university and the mayor of the city helped to reduce the embarrassment of the situation for the library.

These minor incidents were overshadowed by the one major problem which plagued the library over the years. The library had moved to the Dickey Building in 1875, and as early as 1877 Poole was describing the quarters as unsatisfactory. As the rooms were located on the third and fourth floors, it required a long climb to reach them, they were not safe from the danger of fire, and they soon became inadequate to contain the collection or to allow proper space to such important services as the reference department. After several years of negotiation failed to obtain the site of the old post office for a library building, the eyes of the board turned toward the site of old Fort Dearborn, where the city owned property given it by the federal government. Since the terms of the gift seemed to prohibit the erection of any building, the library began to campaign to get Congress to authorize the construction of a library building there. As soon as this plan became known, other groups in the city sought to be included in the terms of the enabling law, since, their proponents said, the library did not need so large a space. The various conflicting claims made the difficult task of getting Congressional approval even more troublesome. Poole was disturbed at the prospect that Dearborn Park might have to be shared. He pointed out that the library was already growing rapidly and that, with suitable quarters, it would attract many gifts which would make its growth even more rapid. Simple arithmetic demonstrated that the library would be very large in only a moderate number of years. It would be foolhardy, he said, to build on half of the Dearborn Park lot if there were not assurance that the rest of it would be available for later expansion.

The campaign for Congressional approval extended over several years. On at least one of those occasions Poole testified formally before the Congressional committee, and on another he spent considerable time in Washington lobbying for the bill. Finally, an alliance was made with the Grand Army of the Republic by which the veterans' organization would share the space for a period of fifty years, after which control would pass to the library. With so potent a political ally, ultimate passage of the bill was probably assured, but, as an anticlimax to the long campaign, a court ruled that the city had always had the power to build in Dearborn Park. The final arrangements included the agreement with the veterans' organization.

All of these negotiations and maneuverings took many years, and even the final agreement did not produce a building for the library during Poole's time there. Meanwhile, the space in the Dickey Building became less and less satisfactory. As elevators became commonplace, even the healthy were less willing to climb stairs. One group that continued to come was not entirely welcome. A regular clientele of unwashed devotees of the daily newspapers formed the group of "library loafers" which seem to plague every metropolitan public library. Improved ventilation was only partially successful in offsetting the offense to the olfactory senses rising from these people. Assignment of a police officer helped to reduce the nuisance, but this problem was never entirely solved in the Dickey Building. Finally, in 1886, new quarters were found for the library. The move coincided with a climactic period of success in Poole's library career.

X. Association President and Library Leader, 1886-1887

During 1886 and 1887 Poole's professional life afforded him un-usual satisfaction. He became the acknowledged leader, not solely of the libraries of the Middle West and of its foremost library, but also of his professional association. The first supplement to his great *Index* was brought well toward completion. In addition, he was elected president of the American Historical Association and continued the historical studies which had helped to earn him that honor. His own library continued its growth and took a spurt forward as, for the first time, it occupied reasonably satisfactory quarters. This period of great success was capped by Poole's ap-pointment as the founding librarian of what promised to become one of the most distinguished libraries of the nation.

Poole devoted the early part of 1886 to making plans for occupy-ing new quarters to take the place of the inadequate rooms in the Dickey Building. As far back as 1881 there had been talk of mov-ing the library to the seat of the municipal government; with the completion of a new city hall, the move seemed more attractive. At last, late in the spring of 1886, the transfer was made.

The change was a substantial improvement even though it provided only a little more space than the library had occupied before. The rooms on the fourth floor of the municipal building at Adams and LaSalle Streets had good lighting, not only because they were higher than the adjoining buildings, but also because they were equipped with the new "Edison incandescent electric lamps." [1] No longer did the patrons have to climb stairs; the li-brary was served by eight elevators, two of them making no stops at intervening floors. Although the seventeen rooms made adminis-tration somewhat more difficult and required the employment of more people, it was now possible to assign individual rooms to special activities. Separate rooms were set aside for the medical reference collection and for patents, as well as more space for administrative and processing functions. The most important addition, however, was the provision of large and pleasant quarters for the reference department. This service, which had grown in importance from year to year, had never before had satisfactory accommodations. In order to provide for the expansion of most services, it was necessary to eliminate others. It was decided to cease to make current American newspapers available, although important ones were preserved for binding. Foreign newspapers continued to be supplied. The choice for omission turned out to be an excellent one, for the undesirables who had made the library their headquarters now ceased to appear. The move and rearrangements took six weeks to complete and were finished just in time for the visit of the delegates to the American Library Association meeting in Milwaukee.

Poole had said that he would not ask the association to visit Chicago while the library occupied its old quarters. With the meeting in Milwaukee, however, he could not refuse to receive the visitors, and he worked feverishly to have the new building ready. The arrangements were completed the day before the delegates arrived. Then the weather played Poole false by producing one of the hot summer days that can make Chicago unbearable. The visitors arrived at midnight and got little rest during the sticky night. The next day they were dutifully shown the wheat pit at the Board of Trade and then the new library. Mayor Carter H. Harrison greeted them cordially and tried to ease the discomfort by speaking of Chicago's cool nights. Having just sweltered through one of them, the librarians were hardly convinced, but the situation was saved somewhat by a pleasant evening's entertainment at Poole's home in cooler Evanston. The next day they went off to Milwaukee where Poole presided over the meetings and delivered his first presidential address.

The subject of Poole's address was the association—its history, its accomplishments, and its future. In it he gave many points of his credo of librarianship and of life. The association, he said, had encouraged efficient and intelligent management, established the soundness of cooperation as a way to produce a bibliographical work, helped to bring about close relationships between public libraries and public schools, and educated the people to the principle of public support for libraries. With all that had been done, much remained. Poole mentioned as most pressing the reform of library architecture, the simplification of classification, and a solution to the problem of the heavy costs of printed catalogs. These needs, he said, did not exhaust the list of the present difficulties, and no one should fear that, once these were solved, others would not take their place. Poole's address ended with a note of personal sadness. Only the previous week he had been shocked by news of the sudden death of his beloved friend, Lloyd Pearsall Smith of the Philadelphia Library Company. It was said of Poole that his character was "formed for friendship" and this loss touched him deeply.[2] He had prepared a warm and graceful tribute to his friend, but he got only as far as the mention of Smith's death before he was overcome with emotion. Turning away from the rostrum, he handed his manuscript to a colleague, who completed the reading for him.

Poole's address at Milwaukee was a revealing statement of his philosophy. Nowhere did he better express his personal warmth, his mellow view of life, his undaunted recognition that problems were endless, or his zest for meeting them as they came. After a long, exhausting, and extremely satisfactory post-conference excursion through Wisconsin and Minnesota, he returned to the problems of his library in its new quarters.

Not satisfied with a new central building, the Chicago Public Library opened the seventh and eighth delivery stations during the next year. Although these new stations helped to bring the circulation to a new high of 627,000 volumes, the central library itself issued more than 500,000 of these books. Not only had circulation increased, but the reference services were more used than ever before. Although the time would soon come when more space in the city hall would be needed, the new quarters brought many benefits to the library. The improved order possible with adequate space was reflected in the annual inventory, which showed the smallest number of missing books ever reported. The prospects for further improvement were bright, especially because the appropriation for 1887–88 was almost $82,000, the largest in the history of the institution up to that time.

In the midst of these favorable prospects, Poole continued his work. Then, one day in the middle of July, 1887, he announced to a group of friends and associates assembled in his office the news that he had just accepted the offer of the trustees of the Newberry estate to make him their librarian. In his resignation, formally submitted on July 23, he said:

In view of the object and magnitude of that noble bequest, and of the importance and responsibility of the position, I have not felt that I could decline it. My tastes and much of my work in years past have been in the direction of organizing libraries, and after forty years of library experience, it seems to be my duty, as it is my inclination, to accept, as I already have done, the very honorable position which has been tendered to me by the Trustees of the Newberry Fund.[3]

The appointment was approved in Chicago. The public library's directors themselves spoke of their

high appreciation of Mr. Poole's scholarly attainments, his thorough acquaintance with bibliography, and Library work, and his untiring devotion to the interests of the Library. By his knowledge of books and the wants of the public, together with his general plan of Administration, he has brought the Library to the high rank which it now holds among the libraries of the country and the great popularity which it has earned among our own citizens.

They expressed their good wishes and their hope that "his latest years will be his best in his chosen profession." [4] The *Tribune* commented that Poole "brings to his new position ample experience," and, after summarizing his career, concluded: "It is gratifying to know that in leaving the Public Library he is going to work for Chicago, though in another institution." [5] All in all, the choice, Poole said, "seems to give *much satisfaction in this latitude*." [6] The congratulations must have come from all over the country, but few could have been more enthusiastic than the one from his friend and former assistant, Charles Evans: "Hurrah! Hurrah! Hurrah! . . . It is a fitting crown to your life work. 'The last, the noblest, and the best.' Please accept my warmest, heartiest, sincerest congratulations." [7]

Others, too, gave their approval. Richard Garnett of the British

Museum, writing in the *Athenaeum,* said: "The trustees . . . have taken the best means of securing a judicious selection of books and efficient library arrangements in general by the appointment." [8] Perhaps, in a sense, the most appreciated congratulations came from the venerable bibliographer, Samuel Austin Allibone. To him, Poole replied:

Nobody can appreciate better than you the responsibilities of the position. As I did not seek the appointment, I feel that, in the Providence of God I have been called to these duties, and I accept them with cheerfulness and zeal. I wish, for this purpose only, that I was a younger man; but I have excellent health, and there is a good deal of work in me yet.[9]

So it was that Poole concluded more than thirteen years of service to the Chicago Public Library. Starting with a collection of fewer than 10,000 books housed in an absurd library structure, he had gone through years of lean budgets and shabby quarters, always optimistic, always looking to better times ahead. And, at last, the better times were coming. Now the library was receiving substantial appropriations each year; it was in new, safe, and clean quarters; it had a staff and an organization which could keep the institution moving ahead. Poole may well have thought, having passed his sixty-fifth birthday, that he was likely to spend the rest of his days at the Chicago Public Library. But now that this new opportunity had come, he greeted it with zest. Back in 1849 he had spoken of his outlook on his existence: "I have ever observed that my capacity for enjoyment increased with my knowledge and my years and I have no fear that now the rule will be reversed." [10] This philosophy seemed to guide his whole life. He looked to the future with confidence. He met each stage of his life with composure. He had some failures, but he was so busy with his next enterprise that he hardly noticed them. Other men might disagree with him; they might criticize. If he thought it worthwhile, he could reply with force. But often it was not worth his time even to answer. And, having had his say, he was content. He had no need to convince the world of his worth, though he enjoyed its praise and its honors when they came. To Poole, life was very good. It had its problems, and, as he had said of the problems of a library, when one was solved, there would be another awaiting solution. But a man was born, matured, and grew old. Each stage and all its hazards were a part of life and so were good. He had no regrets. He did not wish to have his youth back—except for one thing. The opportunity and the challenge of the Newberry Library appealed to him. For that, and that alone, he would have liked to have more time. But, never mind, he was not dead yet. There was much to do, and he would do as much of it as he could.

Poole did not wait to begin working on the problem of the Newberry Library. Even while he was still at the Chicago Public Library, he was busy preparing lists of the books he would need, the fine old books which listed other books. But before he could get very far with that task, he had another assignment. He was president of the American Library Association, and, regardless of any new commitments, he must go to its meeting.

Poole went to the Thousand Islands conference of the American Library Association in as favorable a situation as could be imagined. He was the chief officer of his professional association. Though not the longest career among librarians of the day, his professional life had been very long indeed and had included the leadership of some of the greatest libraries of the nation. Now he was embarking on a new course in an institution which bore promise of overshadowing most of the others of its type. When Poole, with his wife, boarded the train in Chicago, he must have felt satisfied indeed. Arriving at Round Island, where the conference was to be held, he was greeted, no doubt, with congratulations from all sides. Again this year, he delivered an address.

"The Public Library of Our Time" was Poole's valedictory as a public librarian. His own career had coincided closely with the rise of the public library as an institution. Serving first in social libraries, he had turned to the municipally supported institutions after the Civil War, playing a part in the founding of several such libraries and setting the floundering Cincinnati Public Library firmly on its feet. He had then turned to the infant Chicago Public Library and made it the large and healthy organization that it was in 1887. No other man in the country had served so long and varied a career at the head of important public libraries. Now that he was about to leave the field, it was particularly fitting that he should review the public library movement in a formal address.

Poole began with a reiteration of his classic definition of the public library, a term which, he regretted, was not so well understood as the phrase "public school" to refer to "a municipal institution, established and regulated by State laws, supported by local taxation, and administered for the benefit of all the residents of the municipality." The institution, Poole said, had "come into being within the memory of some of us here present," and its rise illustrated the rapid growth of popular education during the century.

Public collections for scholars, he said, were not new, going back at least as far as the Egyptians. National, university, and other research libraries had existed in Europe for centuries. These institutions had their own place and function, but the public library's peculiar mission was to serve "the people at large." Some, to be sure, had assembled resources for the scholar as well, but this was not their primary function.

Having talked in general terms of the public library's mission, Poole sketched the history of the movement in England and in the United States. In particular, he spoke of the influence of George Ticknor in determining the special emphasis given at the inception of the Boston Public Library to popular reading as an essential part of a public library's function. After showing by a review of state laws how widespread the institution had become, Poole predicted its continued growth wherever popular education was a matter of public interest.

Poole's paper contended that all libraries grow hand in hand. The public library was not a deterrent to other libraries; on the contrary, the phenomenal growth of the British Museum, the Library of Congress, and Harvard College Library had been contemporaneous with the rise of the public library. As an illustration, he cited the experience of the Athenaeum and the Boston Public Library, telling how Ticknor had sought to merge the two institutions and how the elder Quincy had made the dramatic plea in Freeman Chapel which had saved his beloved proprietary library. The result, Poole said, had been that the Athenaeum had flourished as never before, though "within a rifle-shot range" of the public library.

In his remarks, Poole did not mention the Newberry Library by name, but there can be no doubt that he was thinking not alone of Boston but of Chicago when he concluded his address by pointing out that the experience of the Athenaeum and the Boston Public Library was "a practical illustration of the support which a popular library and a reference library in the same community give to each other." [11]

After Poole's return to Chicago, he had one more duty to perform for the benefit of the public library. He was already busy, of course, with his new assignment, but he also did his utmost to see that his old place was filled by a man who would take good care of the institution he had built. No sooner had his resignation been announced than the politicians decided to take the job for one of their loyal supporters. The Chicago library, according to newspaper accounts, had not been free of patronage problems. Although the Illinois law allowed no more than one city council representative at a time to serve on the library board, the members were, after all, nominated by the mayor and confirmed by the council. Appointment to the board was hardly a large plum, but it was one way to reward the faithful. Since the Committee on Administration had the power to recommend appointees, library jobs had not always been dispensed on the basis of merit alone. Now that the chief executive's position was available, the Republicans thought they saw an opportunity. The fight soon settled down to a contest between Thomas C. MacMillan, a Republican stalwart who had served on the library's board from 1882 to 1887, and Frederick H. Hild, Poole's office assistant, who, in twelve years, had become a highly capable librarian. The issue became one of patronage versus civil service. The board split evenly, four on each side, and the deciding vote was in the hands of a board member who was in Europe. Finally, in the middle of October, he returned and cast the deciding vote in Hild's favor.

With Hild's appointment, the Chicago Public Library was protected from falling wholly into the hands of the politicians. In the years which followed, the library grew to fulfill some of the promise Poole had seen for it. Provision of additional space in the city hall made it possible for the library to remain there until, in 1897, it could occupy its impressive new building. The Chicago

Public Library, set on its course by Poole's thirteen-year administration, grew to be a great and flourishing institution. But, though Poole naturally kept his interest in it, he had new challenges to command his attention.

XI. Newberry Library: Acquiring a Collection

The Newberry Library was the product of the bequest of Walter Loomis Newberry, a pioneer Chicago banker and businessman whose fortune came largely from spectacular rises in the value of his extensive real-estate holdings. When he died in 1868, he left life interests in his estate for his wife and two daughters, but only if his daughters married and had children was the estate to go to his descendants; otherwise half the estate would be distributed to his nieces and nephews, and the other half would go to found a library. When the second daughter died without heirs in 1876, the operation of the contingency clause became assured, but the will provided that it should not take effect until after the death of the widow. Finally, with Mrs. Newberry's death in 1885, the division of the estate could be made, but the many details of appraisal and settlement took time. At last, on July 1, 1887, the trustees formally created the institution under the name "The Newberry Library." As of the date of Mrs. Newberry's death, the estate was appraised at $4,298,403.20, giving the library $2,149,201.60. This sum yielded a substantial income, although the rate of return was low since so much of the estate consisted of real property. The trust was land-poor, but the time had come to form the library, and the trustees proceeded to their task.

On July 11 the trustees decided that the site of the library would be the block occupied before the Fire by the Newberry residence. Two days later they appointed Poole to be their librarian. He took up his duties on August 1. In the new position Poole was the servant of the trustees. Newberry had specified only that the library should be free and open to the public and that it should be located in the "North Division" of the city. All other matters were left to the discretion of the trustees. Their background made them tend toward conservatism.

The senior and clearly dominant trustee was Eliphalet Wickes Blatchford. He, like most of the civic leaders of the time, had come to Chicago from the East. A successful manufacturer of lead products, he combined with his civic and philanthropic activities a hard-bitten business approach to the affairs of the Newberry Library. It was difficult for him to understand that there were differences between the operation of a library and the running of his business. Although he was only sixty-one, his participation in the affairs of his company had begun to slacken. Thus, he had time available to devote to the library. After 1871, when Mark Skinner, Newberry's lawyer and confidential adviser, resigned his trusteeship, Blatchford's new associate was William Henry Bradley.

Bradley was a man of different character. He too had come from the East, but, rather than enter the busy commercial life as Newberry and Blatchford had done, he had served for many years as clerk of the United States District Court in Chicago. In that capacity he had been responsible for very large amounts of money deposited with the court. He was a man admired not only for his wisdom and judgment but for his kindness and geniality. Already seventy-one, he was a quiet and gentle soul who left many of the hard, unpleasant duties to his more assertive colleague.

If the trustees, with Blatchford in the lead, kept a firm hand on the reins, it was no more than they felt to be their duty. They had the management not only of a library but of a large and complex estate. Each of them received $5,000 annually for his services, and they proposed to earn their pay. They made the appointments, approved the purchases, paid the bills, and took care of all the business affairs. Nor did they stop there. On one occasion Blatchford became so impatient while watching the janitor work that he seized the broom and demonstrated the proper way to sweep a floor. No area of the library's operation was beyond their reach, for they were responsible for it all. In the exercise of their duties they had, in a period of a month, created and set in motion a new institution. On August 6 they provided the financial means to operate it by appropriating $40,000 for the purchase of books and $10,000 for other expenses. The Newberry Library was in business.

The keynote for the first years of the library's existence was expressed in one of Poole's first official acts when, on August 8, he sent off to B. F. Stevens two lists of bibliographical works, one English and one continental European, to be procured for the library. The German list was sent to Otto Harrassowitz in Leipzig. These two men served as principal agents for the Newberry. Stevens was a competent agent and an old friend, though Poole did not let friendship stand in the way of prompt complaint when there were discrepancies in a shipment or other difficulties. There was a healthy frankness, tolerance, and trust between the librarian and the English dealer. Harrassowitz soon demonstrated the competence which called from Poole the praise: "He is very intelligent, prompt, and at the same time prudent, and always looking after our interests." [1]

Other dealers served the Newberry in addition to these two. Purchases of current American books were made primarily from A. C. McClurg and Company of Chicago. American periodical orders were placed for years with a firm known as the Subscription News Company. Later, Gustav E. Stechert began to receive orders with some regularity. Spanish and Latin American dealers were a despair to Poole, as they have been to librarians ever since:

I know nothing, could never find out anything, and have abandoned long since the idea of having, or desiring, any communication with them. . . . The men I have tried to do business with in those countries have no idea of business. They answer letters when they get ready; and their study seems to be how big a swindle we will stand in this particular transaction.

This opinion did not apply to dealers in Europe, though Poole knew there were "book sharks" there also:

I know some of them, and give them a wide berth. I know their methods, one of which is to offer low commissions, and so low that the work cannot be done without cheating in some other way. We employ agents who charge fair commissions, and do not cheat. We find it profitable to buy Spanish and Spanish-American books through these houses.[2]

Over the years the Newberry Library ordered from other dealers from time to time, but the fine old European works were bought mainly from Harrassowitz and Stevens. At the outset the orders were almost exclusively for those works which would be needed in preparing lists of books to be acquired and in cataloging them.

The first Stevens list was a very rich one, including works like Brunet, Larousse, Lorenz, Quérard, Lowndes, Watt, and Halkett and Laing. The selection showed the character and the delights of the task which Poole had ahead of him. He was only beginning to assemble a library which was to be composed of the best books of the past. He could seek fresh copies of titles which had been around him all of his working life. To seek them anew was like meeting old friends. Nor, at that point, did he have to make hard choices. He knew thousands of books which it was only necessary to call to mind to know that he wanted them. Many he had only to list to have Stevens produce them for him. His problem with Stevens was not in failure to get the books; on the contrary, Stevens looked with a relish only partly commercial at the prospect of supplying treasures of the literary world to the library which his old friend was assembling. Poole patiently explained that the library had as yet little room for books: "When you come to understand the purposes of the Trustees you will be glad as I am to conform to them." [3]

Poole, too, had difficulty in restraining himself. That first autumn he was tempted by the special opportunity created by the sale of Americana collected by Charles H. Guild, and he went off to Boston, where he bought 3,000 of the 5,000 lots offered. On his way home he stopped off in New York to attend some other sales. In the one trip he acquired nearly as many books as the small, rented suite of offices at 90 LaSalle Street would hold.

Books were acquired not only by purchase through dealers like Stevens and Harrassowitz and at auction but from individuals as well. The fact that he had such a wide circle of acquaintances enabled Poole to get many reports and documents as gifts. Indeed, ten years before he had been responsible for the gift of the first book presented to the library. In 1877, as a feature of the Caxton anniversary celebration, one hundred copies of the Bible were printed at the Oxford University Press, bound in London, and delivered for exhibit, all within twelve hours. Twenty copies of the Caxton Memorial Bible were to be sent to the United States. When Poole was in England in the fall to attend the London Conference of Librarians, he asked Henry Stevens, who was in charge of the distribution, to give a copy for the Newberry Library. The volume had been kept in a vault for ten years, awaiting the creation of a library to house it. After the library was founded, many other gifts were presented. The Boston Public Library sent its catalogs, including those of its Barton Shakespeare collection and its Ticknor Spanish Library. The trustees of the Peabody Institute of Baltimore sent the important catalog of that library. Individuals and institutions around the country made many donations to the promising young library.

As was to be expected, the Newberry received many letters from persons seeking to sell books from their private collections. Poole replied carefully to these offers. His regularly reiterated policy was to insist that the seller set his own price. Poole's reason for this rule was stated in reply to a suggestion by a colleague that he name his own price for an offered run of a periodical:

You place too much confidence in me in making me set the price of your partial file of the *Anti-Slavery Standard*. I have great confidence in my ability as an appraiser and my impartiality; but I have not enough of the aforesaid qualities to execute the commission you would intrust [*sic*] to me. I see here an opportunity of making shipwreck of what reputation I have in that line. I can easily satisfy myself; but am sure I could not satisfy you. . . . If I should make you an offer, the amount would take away your breath for awhile, and you might expire with apnoea. You are a useful man, and I want you to live many years yet.[4]

Occasionally, when a seller continued reluctant, Poole would make an offer, being careful to state that he did so only as an exception to the rule and to specify the basis on which he reached the price, usually the sum for which the book had been listed in a dealer's catalog or the amount it had brought at auction. By such private negotiation, by auction purchases, by orders to dealers, and by gifts and exchanges, the Newberry Library acquired its collection.

Although, at the outset, purchases were limited to the tools needed by the library in its work and to those other books that Poole could not resist, the policies to be followed in building a collection began to take shape. The Newberry would begin by buying the books needed by working scholars. Ultimately, the library would want the expensive books sought by connoisseurs of fine illustration, binding, and printing. But, for the time, even after there was space, the collecting efforts would be concentrated upon the books useful for a working collection. The criterion of usefulness did not mean that the library would have only elementary books. It was to be a research library for the serious and mature scholar. The purpose was

to provide for the wants of scholars, scientific students, professional men, who want to get below the surface, and inquire into the origin and history of ideas and progress of events—who read and seek for books in many languages.[5]

When the time came to select books for the scholars' working collection, Poole sought the advice and assistance of subject specialists. The most notable instance of the early years was the participation of George B. Upton, distinguished music critic and author. Upton himself took the initiative in suggesting that the Newberry collect intensively in the field of music and compiled a comprehensive list of books to be purchased. He was one who offered his services. On other occasions Poole took advantage of complaints about lacks in the collection to suggest that the complainant help select books to fill the gaps. And, going a step further, he took the initiative himself in seeking assistance. Poole felt qualified to select a few thousand books for a public library, but he was aware that he did not know enough about the literature of the whole range of knowledge to recommend the obscure but important works in each field. And, too, the prestige of an outside scholar would carry weight with the trustees who, by intent, if not always literally, reviewed every purchase before it was made. "The rule is that I report to the Trustees, and they authorize or not the purchase, usually, however, confirming my recommendations." [6]

The necessity of consulting the trustees closely on book purchases was sometimes a trial to Poole. The procedure was not at all new to him. The Athenaeum's committee had been active in supervising purchases, and even in the public libraries the boards had the controlling voice. But Poole had always been skillful in obtaining the confidence of his various supervising committees. Especially in the Chicago Public Library, he had been the experienced professional dealing with a regularly changing group of laymen. Underlying any informal understandings, however, was the fact that the board, whether in a public institution or a private one, was the responsible and the ruling body. No matter how much confidence and consent Poole might be able to gain, he knew and did not question that the board's word was final. There might be authority delegated to him, and, within that area, he might point out to the board members, if challenged, that the matter was presumably his responsibility, but there was never any doubt that the power of delegation included the power of recall. To Poole the librarian of an institution was an employee of that institution and subject to the absolute authority of its governing body in official matters. Still, the reins could chafe at times.

Early in the first year Barton at the Antiquarian Society offered a set of the Massachusetts Historical Society *Collections* at $150. Poole considered it a good buy, and Blatchford agreed to the purchase. It is easy to imagine a conversation in which Blatchford suggested that they seek a discount, Poole protested that the Antiquarian Society was not a book dealer to be haggled with, and Blatchford insisted that it would do no harm to try. Whatever the exact conversation, the resulting correspondence remains. Poole wrote to Barton reciting the offer and adding: "If in naming that price you had in mind to make a discount of 10 percent, the Trustees will not object." This attempt at close dealing was too much for Poole to take on his own head. He added a "Personal":

I understood the price you named to be *net;* and I made the inquiry about discount, at the request of one of the Trustees who is a *business* man. I am sometimes happy that I have not been trained as a *business* man.[7]

Fortunately, Blatchford never heard about this bit of treasonable insubordination.

In 1889 the trustees had difficulty in bringing themselves to spend the money for an exceptionally rich collection, although it was offered by the owner at a bargain price in order to have it kept together. When the owner became restive at the trustees' delay, Poole wrote to him as an old personal friend, saying that he would

venture to give the opinion that, being very busy men, they will require more time in coming to a decision than you may think necessary and reasonable. I hope, therefore, that you will be as patient as you can be conveniently while the negociations [*sic*] are going on. Please also consider that they are not so familiar as you are in large book-buying transactions. Hoping that you will give the Trustees the time they need. . . .[8]

If, at times, Poole could not contain himself when the trustees were more close-fisted than he thought proper, he could also ease and smooth their way.

Working under the close supervision of the trustees, Poole assembled books for the library. Early in 1888, when the library moved to new quarters, he could begin to buy books in earnest. Once that space was overflowing with books, the library moved to another and larger building especially constructed to serve until the permanent building was completed. Thus, after only a brief wait, the library was able to embark on its purchasing essentially unimpeded by lack of space.

The choice of books followed, in large part, the policy which Poole had stated at the beginning. One of the most notable concentrations was the purchase of basic scholarly sets. Examples of the sets purchased during the next few years were the *Publications* of the Early English Text Society, Hansard's *Debates, Annales de Chimie* in 309 volumes and the scarce *Astronomische Nachrichten* in 135, the *Corpus Scriptorum Historiae Byzantinae* in 55 volumes, and Petitot's *Collection des Mémoires relatifs à l'Histoire de France* in 130. Works of similar or even greater importance were added in considerable quantity year after year. It was natural that in a library headed by Poole special efforts were made to acquire the periodicals included in his *Index* as well as the basic works relating to the history of America, such as the collections of the state historical societies and accounts of the voyages of the early explorers.

Despite the professed intention to wait until later to acquire rarities, a number of them were bought from time to time, such as Luther's New Testament (1522) and Old Testament (1523), the King James Bible (1611), several first editions of Milton, and a magnificent copy of Prince Maximilian zu Wied's *Voyage dans l'Intérieur de l'Amérique du Nord*. Some of the rarities were acquired as a result of the acquisition of entire collections. Early in the history of the library, Count Pio Resse offered his music collection to the trustees, and, after considerable soul-searching, they decided to buy it. This fine collection included among its treasures the music of the first opera performed in public, Jacopi Peri's *Euridice* (1600), together with the original libretto of the same date. This purchase, together with the works bought separately on Upton's recommendation, gave the Newberry at once one of the outstanding music collections in the country.

In 1890 the library made a purchase which made up for its slow beginning in collecting rarities. Henry Probasco of Cincinnati had decided in the middle of 1889 to sell his notable private library. He turned immediately to his old friend Poole who, twenty years earlier, had advised him on its arrangement and had secured the services of two former Athenaeum librarians to catalog it. Poole knew an opportunity when he saw one, and he wrote a carefully worded letter of encouragement, appealing to Probasco's personal pride, to his interest in scholarship, and to his affection for the collection which he had painstakingly assembled:

I hardly need assure you—in case you have fully made up your mind to sell—that it would give me great personal satisfaction to have it come to the Newberry Library *en bloc*.

It seems a pity to break up such a collection. Here it would attract a good deal of attention, and would be fully appreciated. It would also associate the name of the collection in an interesting and honorable way with the organization and history of the Newberry Library. This Library, with three million dollars behind it, you are probably aware is to be for the use of scholars and not for the circulation of books; and will be the great reference library of the West.

The story of the British Museum cannot be mentioned without bringing up the names of Sir Hans Sloane and Sir Robert Bruce Cotton. About twenty years ago the wonderfully complete Shaksperian collection of Thomas P. Barton . . . was bought by the Boston Public Library; and the *Barton Collection* is, and always will be, known to scholars the world over. . . . The Probasco collection, if it came entire to the Newberry Library, would be conspicuous among its treasures.

My thoughts for some time have been running in this direction; and I now frankly express them in this personal and confidential letter. If they meet a favorable response from you I will bring them to the attention of the Trustees. They have not been inclined, thus far, to buy entire libraries, believing that the money could be employed more usefully in selecting books from different collections, and thus avoiding the purchase of duplicates. The only instance in which they have varied from this method was in buying the collection of Count Resse,

the books being offered at a price which seemed to make it an object.
Mrs Barton, in order that the library . . . might be kept together
as a memorial of him, offered it to the Trustees of the Boston Public
Library at a price less than she could probably have realized at public sale, and the Trustees bought it. I have a feeling that the Trustees
of the Newberry Library may be inclined, if the opportunity is offered
them, to act with reference to your library, as the Trustees of the
Boston Public Library acted with reference to the Barton Collection.

If you do not readily fall in with the views I have suggested, please
say so, and I will let the matter drop.[9]

Thus began the negotiations for the acquisition of what was to be
one of the Newberry's notable collections. The letter was a most
felicitous example of Poole's ability to be direct and open and yet
delicate in conveying the financial aspect of the matter.

The negotiations did not lead immediately to the purchase.
The trustees considered the matter slowly and carefully, with the
result that Poole had his hands full keeping Probasco's patience
from being exhausted. Finally, after visiting Cincinnati to see the
books, the trustees concluded that they could not afford the purchase. Probasco then turned the collection over to Robert Clarke,
the Cincinnati book dealer and publisher, on consignment. Clarke
renewed negotiations with the Newberry, and, finally, the trustees
were persuaded to buy. As conservative men, they did not find it
easy to part with $52,924. Although the price was a very substan-
tial sum, the collection was a bargain. Probasco sold at two thirds
of his original expenditure. Audubon's *Birds* cost the Newberry
$733.33, the Shakespeare folio of 1623, $800.00, and the folio of
1632, $197.33. In later years only a few of the nuggets would have
returned the cost of the whole collection. It was an assemblage of
books to delight the eyes and heart of a connoisseur. When the
books arrived, Poole could not contain his pleasure at seeing and
handling them.

The 404 examples of art binding covered three centuries of
craftsmanship, highlighted by 2 autographed Groliers. Among the
other delights of the 2,500 volumes were 88 rare Bibles, including
the first and second King James Bibles of 1611, thus duplicating
one of the earlier purchases. Then there were the first, second,
and fourth Shakespeare folios; 10 editions of Homer, beginning
with the Aldine of 1517; 9 editions of Dante, from 1477; 8 of

Horace, including the Aldine of 1519; and the elephant-folio edition of Audubon's *Birds* and the folio of his *Quadrupeds*. These examples were only some of the brightest of a sumptuous collection. The purchase was not greeted with unanimous praise. One newspaper spoke of "antique lard cans" [10] in criticizing the trustees for their action. It was certainly true that the Newberry could have bought many other books if they had declined the Probasco collection, but it was also an opportunity that could come only once. Poole thought it a wise purchase. Indeed, assuming that the Newberry should have been collecting great rarities at all, there can be no doubt of its wisdom.

Another collection begun in 1890 was notable for its objective of service to an influential group in the community rather than for its rarities. Early in the year the trustees agreed to the requests of the Medical Library Association and of individual physicians that the Newberry accept responsibility for assembling and maintaining a medical library. Efforts to establish such a collection in the public library had never produced results satisfactory to the medical men. After an unsuccessful venture to provide for the need themselves, they turned to the Newberry Library. The collections from both the public library and the Medical Library Association were brought together in the Newberry Library, and the new collection was launched.

The acceptance of this responsibility and the transfer of books from the public library were in line with statesmanlike pronouncements made by the trustees at about that time in connection with the beginning of another reference library. With the death of John Crerar late in 1889, the city was assured of having a collection on the South Side to match the Newberry in the north. The trustees suggested that it would be well for the principal libraries of the city to divide the fields of emphasis. The public library should concentrate upon the sort of books which could be borrowed, while the Newberry, as a reference library, should obtain the more expensive works appropriate to its own specialization. The public library's fine patent collection would take care of the city's needs. The Newberry's music collection need not be duplicated elsewhere. In many subjects one good collection would be sufficient. "To this end it is desirable that there be a concert of action between [the] Trustees of the three libraries, and that an allotment be made of the special fields they will cover in their collections." [11] In this fashion the trustees of the Newberry Library, just as their librarian had done fourteen years before, called those charged with the care of the city's libraries to embark upon a course of cooperation and not competition. The prospects were good that this policy would prevail, for among the twelve trustees named in Crerar's will was E. W. Blatchford.

Poole heartily approved of the idea of cooperative division of subjects among the various libraries, but, as he later explained, he meant the division to apply primarily to the more specialized and expensive works. The Newberry Library, he said, must have

full apparatus for the general student. Its departments of history, biography, travels, popular science, bibliography, sets of literary periodicals, dictionaries, encyclopaedias, and reference books, as well as general literature, must be kept up without reference to the fact that the same books are in the other libraries; for they will be in constant demand by readers.

The description of the Newberry as a "reference" library, Poole said, meant more than simply that the books might not be taken for home use. Rather, the word "characterizes the purpose, nature and constitution of the Library itself." The institution should be "primarily for the use of earnest and advanced students; or, in other words, to be a scholars' Library." [12]

It is doubtful that Poole meant to restrict the Newberry to a relatively few fields as fully as was eventually done. He was, in fact, reluctant to leave out anything completely. In a list of 276 subjects which he prepared for the trustees, he left only 3—law, patents, and popular fiction—to be cared for exclusively by other libraries. On the other hand, 206 were to be considered as subjects for collecting on a general level only. The remaining 67 topics were to be the "Departments of Special Interest." Except for 8 topics in science and technology, these subjects were in line with the later specializations of the Newberry Library, being concentrated in bibliography and fine printing, biography and history, language and literature, fine arts, and political science.[13] It is likely, however, that Poole would have included rather extensive collections in the subjects of general interest. He expected the

Newberry to become a much larger library than it actually did. He was opposed to great selectivity in collecting and to the practice of "weeding" a collection. Though he would agree that not every book was appropriate to every collection, he maintained that a book which in one library was a weed might be in another library an exotic flower of great value. In Poole's later years at the Newberry, the difference in conception in his mind and in the minds of the trustees became a source of disagreement. Especially as the permanent building began to require large sums of money, the trustees became more and more convinced that they must limit their expenditures for books to current income and must restrict the fields of collecting accordingly. The trustees were also aiming at immediate usefulness for the library, whereas Poole, not unmindful of immediate needs, thought of the work being done as the mere foundations of a very large collection. In Poole's thinking the collecting policy should be set in terms of years; to the trustees the goals should be kept more modest and more immediate. Yet the trustees' conception covered a broad range of subjects and, in terms of available income, was probably more realistic than Poole's idea.

Despite the breadth of Poole's conception, the books bought during his librarianship were, in general, well adapted to the needs of the Newberry and laid solid foundations for its later, more specialized growth. Although he said that it was his custom "to regard books not from my personal preferences, but through the preferences of readers," it is not surprising that the major fields built up during those years were in the historical and humanistic studies, which were his own particular interests. During the seven years of his tenure the library acquired some 120,000 books and 44,000 pamphlets at a cost which was probably close to $250,000. Its major strengths were bibliography and rare books, history, music, and language and literature. Perhaps most significant for the future development of the library were the extensive purchases of basic scholarly sets and serials which, with the specialized monographs in each field, were the "distinctive feature of a great Reference Library." [14] Under Poole's administration the Newberry Library acquired a collection which was impressive in itself and which laid the ground for future growth.

XII. Newberry Library:
Planning a Building

In 1882 Poole had said that, when the time came to erect a building for the Newberry Library, "one of the most interesting problems in library construction which have occurred in this country will then present itself." [1] He could hardly have known that he himself would be the one to plan a solution to that problem, but it was a challenge for which he had been preparing himself for years.

Poole had been one of the leading spokesmen in the American Library Association on the subject of buildings. As early as 1876, in a statement which could have served as an outline for instructions to the architect of the Newberry Library, he gave in essence his final conclusions regarding library architecture. In later years he refined and expanded his ideas. In 1881 he gave a formal paper in which he criticized the existing large libraries of the United States and presented a detailed plan illustrating the principles he proposed as improvements. In 1885 he delivered a companion paper giving his ideas of the best solution for a small public library. At other conferences of the association, he reported on new buildings and gave critiques of them. His advice was sought in connection with many buildings, and in some instances he drew up detailed plans, most notably in connection with his service as trustee of Northwestern University, a position to which he was elected in 1891 and in which he served for the remainder of his life. He was a member of the Library Committee during the period when the plans for a university library building were made, and the resulting structure was essentially the one he had recommended for small public libraries in 1885.

The planning for the Newberry Library was Poole's only experience in starting from the beginning on a building for a library that he headed. He had frequently planned the arrangement of space in buildings that already existed, either in fact or in prospect. At the Mercantile Library new quarters were occupied during his tenure. At the Athenaeum substantial rearrangement, reconstruction, and expansion of space had taken place. At Cincinnati part of a new building was occupied, and plans were prepared for the arrangement of the rest of the building then under construction. At Chicago the library was moved three times while he was librarian. The Newberry Library, however, was his only opportunity to carry a building from start to finish.

The building erected for the Newberry Library embodied ideas that had been developing in Poole's mind over the years. The result was not a reproduction of a building which he had seen and in which he had worked. On the contrary, the influence of his past experience was almost wholly in the direction of a reaction against faults which he had found in the older buildings. The result, far from being negative, was a body of ideas which was probably his most original contribution to librarianship. Not until after half a century did these ideas take strong hold. When they did, however, they came to form a dominant feature of library thought, since they embodied not just principles of library architecture but also a basic approach to library organization for service.

The principles which Poole advocated were ahead of his time, not only in relation to libraries but in relation to architecture in general. At a time when only a few rebel architects were advocating functionalism rather than traditionalism, Poole was making such remarks as his comment in 1881 that "the same secular common-sense and the same adaptation of means to ends which have built the modern grain-elevator and reaper are needed for the reform of library construction." [2] This functional approach was evident in his remark that there were fundamental relationships that should be respected in planning libraries just as there were in planning houses. "It is well that the kitchen have a proper relation to the dining-room, and the laundry be not an adjunct to the reception-room." [3] He urged most strongly that library buildings should be planned in their essentials by librarians rather than by architects. "After the inside has been planned in all its details, the architect is brought in to give the creature an artistic dress and out-side covering." [4]

Poole was scornful of architects who slavishly followed tradition at the expense of convenience, creating monuments rather than useful buildings. In 1890, in regard to the Boston Public Library building then under construction, he raised a great stir by pub-licly criticizing "the Italian palace" [5] which the noted architects, McKim, Mead, and White, had planned for Copley Square. In per-haps the most colorful expression of his advocacy of functionalism, he added:

We live in peaceful communities. The skulking Indian has departed. The ministers and deacons have now no occasion to take with them to church their flint-locks and powder-horns. With this change in the times, should there not be a corresponding change in our every-day architecture? In libraries abundant light is more essential than facili-ties for fortification. [6]

In addition to his emphasis on usefulness rather than tradition, Poole took into consideration practical matters of construction methods and the strength of materials. His selection of the width of fifty feet for a reading room was based on the conclusion that this span was the widest which could be supported by iron beams without intervening columns and on the opinion that satisfactory light for reading would penetrate only twenty-five feet from win-dows on either side. With the weight of the structure thus inde-pendent of interior walls, the way was open to a flexible building. In 1885 Poole specified that his proposed small public library have its interior space divided by movable partitions rather than by permanent walls in order that the space could be rearranged to fit changing needs.

The functional building which Poole advocated contained many rooms rather than the dominant great hall which had become tra-ditional. Poole's building thus raised a difficulty in administration. Whatever its defects, a great hall containing the bulk of the book collection could be administered from a central point more easily than could a building with many rooms. The sequence in which Poole presented his ideas suggests that his championship of a new plan of library organization grew mainly from the need to use the building which he proposed, rather than stemming from an already conceived pattern of service. Poole advocated the division of the book collection into a number of subject departments, each occupying a separate room and administered by a librarian whose background included appropriate specialization. But, if the building fundamentally gave inspiration to the plan of service, it was not the sole justification, and Poole soon developed a rationale which gives considerable warrant to the claim which has been made for him as the father of subject departmentalization.[7] It is also true that he had shown a very early interest in subject departments and an appreciation of their usefulness by his creation of a department for fine arts and decoration in Cincinnati. It seems, nevertheless, that his service plan grew primarily from the unorthodox building and that the building itself was basically a reaction against the buildings of the past.

The old-fashioned sort of building which Poole disliked was essentially the Gothic church form with a large, high, open hall surrounded by alcoves on the main floor and in galleries above. This same basic plan was least objectionable when built on a small scale, as in Yale's library where Poole began his work. Even there problems of inadequate light and inconvenient arrangement had arisen. When the plan was followed on a large scale, as at the Boston Public Library, the Astor Library, and the Cincinnati Public Library, all of the difficulties were felt in full measure. He protested:

Why library architecture should have been yoked to ecclesiastical architecture, and the two have been made to walk down the ages *pari passu,* is not obvious, unless it be that librarians in the past needed this stimulus to their religious emotions. The present state of piety in the profession renders the union no longer necessary, and it is time that a bill was filed for a divorce.[8]

The divorce was made necessary, Poole thought, primarily by the great main hall. The Cincinnati building which, though not his plan, was built during his tenure was a prime example of the type. Iron shelves and spiral staircases surrounded a vast open hall and ascended to dizzying heights all the way to the ceiling fifty-five feet from the marble floor. At least one visitor to that library found the mere contemplation of the staircases next to the open void a giddying sight. Poole's criticisms were more practical. As a connoisseur of leather, he was troubled by the heat which accumulated in the upper reaches of the great hall and literally consumed both the book bindings and the paper. "Books," he said, "cannot live where men cannot live." [9] The open space wasted more than half the cubic capacity. Sounds anywhere in the room reverberated throughout it, disturbing patrons at the reading tables. If fire should break out, it would be quickly spread by the natural flue of the hall. In fetching books, not only had the attendants to climb long flights of stairs, but they were always moving around the sides of a parallelogram rather than in direct lines from a center point. And, finally, such high heavy walls were expensive to construct and made additions difficult.

The building that Poole outlined in some detail in 1881 was designed to meet all objections to the traditional plan. The building would be a hollow rectangle, containing at one side a main entrance, a reference collection, and the administrative departments. In the wings would be a series of separate reading rooms. All rooms in the building would be fifteen feet high and fifty feet wide, but their lengths would vary to suit differing needs. Each room, however, would be quite separate from every other in order that each could be a fireproof compartment. Access to them would be provided by an iron corridor around the inside of the quadrangle at each floor.

Such a plan for a library building was revolutionary. Fifteen-foot ceilings were, for that time, low indeed. When one bitter critic complained that fully half of the cubage of these rooms would be wasted, Poole replied scornfully that the purpose was to allow the entrance of light and the dissipation of heat. Reacting sharply, as he could when attacked, he added: "The space is there, and only awaits a first-class ignoramus to use it for storing books." [10] Rooms limited to fifteen feet gave little scope for the imposing architectural effects so dear to the hearts of architects, donors, and trustees. Some librarians, too, were reluctant to give up the magnificences made possible by traditional buildings, but most were concerned with the problems of excessive heat, fire hazard, and waste of space, just as Poole was. The plan, however, was Poole's own. Other librarians proposed to achieve some of the same objectives by different methods, primarily the use of the book stack, which, with Justin Winsor's backing, became the leading alternative to the buildings of old.

Winsor's plan, incorporated in Gore Hall at Harvard and followed in most large libraries built after that time, combined two basically separate structures in a single building. The book collection was housed in a book stack which packed the volumes into low-ceilinged rooms on successive floors. The readers, staff, and administration were then housed in a different part of the building. A favorite form for libraries of moderate size was the three-story stack having the delivery desk at the middle floor, so that the attendants never had to go more than one flight up or down at any one time. By isolating the book collection, the book stack provided an economical use of space, allowed temperatures to be kept at a lower level than was possible where readers were accommodated, and made it possible for the rest of the building to be constructed in any style. What usually occurred in fact was that the monumental features were perpetuated in great vaulted reading rooms.

Poole did not approve of book stacks. He considered them prisons for books, subject to some of the criticisms of the great hall in the inevitable accumulation of heat at the top and in the constant need for stair-climbing. He did not say that he would never build a book stack, but he would do so only under dire necessity. "I should not like to go to sea in a bowl; but if it were necessary to go and I could get nothing better, I think I should try it." [11]

At one point in the designing of the Newberry building, it began to look as if Poole might be forced to make his figurative journey. The trustees had started making plans for the building from the very beginning, deciding, even before they appointed Poole, to use the site of the old Newberry residence, which had been destroyed in the Great Fire. They engaged the young Henry Ives Cobb as their architect. Cobb, a partner in the highly successful firm of Cobb and Frost, probably had come to the trustees' attention as the designer of the building for the Chicago Historical Society. By agreement with the trustees, he withdrew from his firm in order to devote himself exclusively to the new library building. During 1888 he visited the leading libraries of the United States, and the next year he and Blatchford went off to Europe.

In writing letters of introduction for Cobb to take on his journeys, Poole took special pains to see that the architect talked to those who would favor Poole's own ideas. In particular, he was eager that Herbert Baxter Adams, professor of history at the Johns Hopkins University, describe plans for the University Extension Movement then under way. In 1887 Adams had presented a paper to the American Library Association urging that public libraries sponsor short courses for adults. The scheme included the provision of special facilities and collections of books for those who took the courses. The idea had appealed to Poole, since it fitted in with his plans for special subject departments. When Cobb visited Baltimore, Poole wrote to Adams, asking him particularly to explain the idea and the required facilities to the architect. Inevitably, however, Cobb also saw Winsor and other advocates of book stacks. When Cobb came to draw sketches for the building, both a grand reading room and book stacks were dominating features.

Poole moved forcefully to counter Cobb's proposals. During the fall of 1889 the two men carried on a vigorous debate in a succession of letters to the trustees. Poole sought outside help; he wrote to President Daniel Coit Gilman of the Johns Hopkins University for his support, and he personally employed an architect to draw up plans embodying his own ideas. Additional support in the debate came in December of 1889 with the publication of a long, anonymous communication in the Chicago *Tribune* urging the trustees to adopt Poole's plan. Although the writer was evidently an admirer, he did suggest that the building Poole had outlined in 1881 had three principal defects: the open balconies— to be used as corridors—around the court, an insufficient number of stairways, and an excessive concern with fireproofing. His detailed modifications, however, were not so important as the fact that his article supported Poole's main position.

The idea of small rooms devoted to the storage of special subjects is beyond all praise. . . . Dr. Poole places no book out of reach of an attendant or reader. . . . There is to be but one attendant in each room as its curator, and the readers, instead of filling out blanks and handing them to an official, will go to the shelves, find what they want, and then seat themselves at the tables provided for them in the full

light of the windows facing on the area. Nothing could be more calculated to get from a library all that it can give.[12]

Whether the article was decisive or not, Poole reported in mid-
January of 1890, two weeks after its appearance:

Plans for the permanent building are now coming on well. Mr Cobb
the architect has surrendered, and I am likely to have my ideas carried out. I have got up a beautiful plan which is likely to go through.[13]

In September, when Poole went to the meeting of the American
Library Association, he carried with him the interior plans which
had been finally approved the previous week. In presenting them,
he said:

It is not easy, when we step out of the beaten track, for a number of
thoughtful persons to concur in adopting a design based on new principles, although each desires to avoid the acknowledged faults of construction in what is known as the conventional library building.[14]

As he described the building, it was clear that the architect had
indeed surrendered. With a few modifications, the structure was
the one Poole had presented in Washington in 1881, although only
the front section would be built at the start. The building would
include one large general reading room and many reading rooms
of moderate size to contain, on free-standing shelves, the books on
specific subjects. The ceiling heights would be sixteen feet on the
first floor, fifteen feet on the second, and fourteen feet on the upper floors. The open iron gallery which had provoked considerable
criticism would be transformed into an interior corridor. Light
would enter through large windows on the south and, on the
north, across the corridor into the reading rooms through large,
high windows on the court. An auditorium and small classrooms
would take care of the needs of the proposed University Extension
groups and of school children whose teachers might bring them to
the library. Private study rooms for scholars would be available
on the upper floors. The part of the building to be constructed
first would have an absolute capacity of one million volumes and
a working capacity of 600,000. One of the most remarkable facts
about the plan was that the exterior appearance was not yet settled.
Evidently, the Newberry Library was, for once, to be a library
building in which interior arrangements and convenience were
to dictate the shape of the structure.

During the next few years construction on the building proceeded. The site was not the old Newberry lot originally set aside for it but a full block fronting on Washington Park and bounded by Clark, Oak, and Dearborn Streets and what came to be called Walton Street. This was the site of the Ogden homestead, the only building in the path of the Fire on the North Side to be saved. In the middle of 1889 the trustees had been enabled to buy this property, which, they said, they had preferred all along. While they regretted the necessity to abandon the associations with the library's donor, they felt it was a decision he would have approved. The Ogden property was conveniently located, having the advantage of being on a main cable-car line and yet away from the dirt and noise of the city's center. That the area of the Newberry homestead would become one of the most desirable parts of Michigan Avenue's shopping district or that Washington Park would become a haven for bums known as Bughouse Square was more than could have been foreseen. During the fall of 1890 the foundations of the new building were laid. The previous April the library had moved into a building especially constructed for it only a block away at Oak and State. This structure was designed to be used while the permanent building was under construction and then to be converted into an apartment house.

Work on the building went well. There were delays caused by some difficulties in obtaining granite and steel, but, on the other hand, an unusually long mild spell during the winter of 1891–92 speeded things along. For three years the walls and interior slowly rose before the interested eyes of the people of Chicago. During the summer of 1893 it was one of the sights of the city for visitors to the Columbian Exposition. Cobb's exterior made it a substantial and imposing structure in a modified Byzantine style. Its granite walls and arched windows gave little hint that the interior was a new departure in large library construction. Poole was not concerned on this point. He was content with the "artistic dress" which Cobb had given his "creature." He took pride in its outer appearance, showing off photographs at meetings of the American Library Association and, on one occasion, before a group of Congressmen in Washington. Finally, in November of 1893, work had progressed far enough that the new building could be occupied. Poole himself would have preferred to wait until the workmen were out of the building and the new furniture and equipment ready, but these were only minor matters in the midst of his great pleasure in occupying the building to which he had devoted so much time and thought and persuasive skill. After only a short time, he reported that "the rooms are delightful and the arrangement of special rooms for special subjects superb," and later that "the department method works as well as I expected, and is highly appreciated by our readers." [15]

So it was that, just as he had made a sound beginning for the library's book collection, he presided over the construction of a building to house it. In addition to these responsibilities, he had also to employ and organize a staff and to administer the library during the seven years of his librarianship.

XIII. Newberry Library: Administering a Library, 1887-1894

During the seven years between 1887 and 1894 Poole served as the executive head of a library which he created. In that time a collection of more than 150,000 books and pamphlets was acquired, a building was planned, constructed, and occupied, a staff of more than thirty people was employed, organized, and trained, and service to the public was begun. Before the end of Poole's librarianship a substantial library enterprise had been set on its way. The accomplishments of those years were achieved despite many problems and as a result of much hard work. In the later years of Poole's tenure he came under attack for what, in the judgment of the trustees, were inadequacies in his administration. This painful end to his career was a personal tragedy for Poole, but hardly a fair judgment on his career as a whole, not the least important part of which was his impressive accomplishment in creating from the beginning a library which was, by 1894, already one of the leading research institutions of the United States.

The beginning in August, 1887, was modest indeed. At first, Poole alone handled the affairs of the new library. In November the first assistant was employed; shortly, others joined the staff. The next April the employees under Poole's direction numbered four, and, by the end of 1888, "our little circle" [1] had grown to include seven people.

At first the Newberry was more a planning and book-buying organization than it was a library. In the offices on LaSalle Street and in the temporary quarters on Ontario Street, occupied from 1888 to 1890, there was not even enough space for the staff and the books. By the middle of 1889 the books were so tightly packed into some rooms that the doors literally bulged. In this situation neither proper arrangement of the collection nor adequate service to patrons was possible. Nor was the collection complete enough to satisfy many needs. One patron complained that he thought "the Newberry was to be an elephant among the libraries." Poole replied: "It doubtless will be, but did you ever hear of a Jumbo being grown in a year?"[2]

Although, during these early years, there was much work to be done, the library had not yet grown so large as to require a formal organization. The allotment of work to each staff member was personal and casual. Poole himself spent much of his time selecting books and planning the building. The rest of the staff was left to keep up with the day-to-day tasks, including the maintenance of a catalog of books received and on order. With the move to the large building at Oak and State in April, 1890, the library entered a new phase. There was now enough space for both staff and books and, in addition, adequate reading rooms for patrons. Once a full range of services was begun, the staff had to be enlarged.

The qualifications sought in candidates for employment at the Newberry Library were different from those required by the public libraries which Poole had administered. Usually he had been satisfied to employ people of intelligence, planning to train them himself; they needed neither previous library training nor special subject background. At the Newberry, however, many of the staff members were expected to become the dispensers of specialized services to students and research workers. The Newberry's relation to a public library should be, in Poole's phrase, "that of a university to a grammar school."[3] Except for those in routine jobs, its employees should have qualifications to suit its exalted position.

It was not easy to find properly qualified people, but there was no shortage of applicants. Indeed, the importunities of those who thought of library work as an easy berth had been such a regular accompaniment to Poole's career that he had developed a standard answer:

As a means of simply earning money, I do not recommend library work. Take up anything else. The prizes in the library profession are few; and only those who have peculiar organizations and immense capacity for application and study can achieve success and a moderate pay.

Poole was not, of course, expressing disillusionment with the profession of librarianship; he added that "librarians predestinated, foreordained, and successful, are the happiest and most contented sort of people, and do not regard money-getting as the chief purpose of existence." [4] He emphasized the negative aspects only in order to discourage the unqualified.

There were two principal groups of suitable candidates: Dewey's library school students and college graduates who could be trained in the Newberry Library itself. Poole employed only a few from the library school. The first employee, Annie E. Hutchins, had attended briefly, but her chief training had been at Harvard under Winsor. Miss Edith E. Clarke came from the position of head cataloger at Columbia to a similar place at the Newberry. George Watson Cole, later the distinguished librarian of the Henry E. Huntington Library, had graduated from the library school. Dr. George Wire's unusual combination of medical training, library school training, and several years' experience at Northwestern University Library made him a logical choice to head the medical collection. Miss Ema K. Hopson came for a few months but soon left to be married. Miss Lydia A. Dexter, Edwin Hatfield Anderson, and Dr. James M. Wilson had all attended the library school without graduating. Miss Dexter and Dr. Wilson stayed for some years, but Anderson left after about ten months to take another position in a career which eventually led him to the head of the New York Public Library.

Although some of the library school recruits achieved prominence in the profession, Poole concluded that such training was by no means essential, saying that library school graduates required "about the same instructions and oversight as persons of scholarly and linguistic attainments who have not had a Library School training." He continued to believe that the place to train librarians was in a library:

Our experience, in employing, at first with a low salary, persons who have had a university training, and are well up in the ancient and modern languages, and furthermore have an ambition to educate themselves in the library profession as a life-work, has been most successful. They become just such workers as we need, and it will be difficult to find their superiors elsewhere.[5]

A number of those who received their early library training at the Newberry later became well known in the profession. Among them were Marilla Waite Freeman, who at her retirement headed the services in the main building of the Cleveland Public Library; William Stetson Merrill, whose *Code for Classifiers* became a standard work of librarianship; and Haakon Nyhuus, who, after additional service at the Chicago Public Library, returned to his native Norway to lead its libraries in adopting American methods, which, in such details as type of classification, physical arrangement of quarters, and establishment of delivery stations, were those developed by Poole at the public library. Other Newberry trainees were Steingrimur Stefánsson, who became chief reviser at the Library of Congress; Charles Martel, who, with J. C. M. Hanson, is given chief credit for devising the Library of Congress classification; and Hanson himself, who eventually returned to join the staff of the University of Chicago Library and the faculty of Chicago's Graduate Library School. In addition to these beginners, the Newberry also employed Charles Evans, who returned to work under his old mentor as he had years before at the Athenaeum. The Newberry Library, under Poole's administration, gave training and experience to a considerable number of people who eventually achieved notable success as librarians.

The very qualifications which the Newberry sought in its staff members could lead to problems at times. William Klapp Williams, one of the early recipients of the Doctor of Philosophy degree from the Johns Hopkins University, was so conscious of his background that he was never satisfied even after he was made head of the classification and reference department. This feeling of inadequate recognition seems to have been a source of the nervous exhaustion which eventually caused him to leave. Miss Clarke finally concluded that she herself would be a good choice to supplant Poole as librarian. Hanson complained that much of his time had been spent simply copying cards rather than in the more responsible work which he preferred. Especially in the early years before the subject departments were ready for full operation, it was difficult to give adequate scope and recognition to the capacities of some of the staff.

Another source of difficulty was the regular intervention of the trustees. On one occasion they listened, without Poole's knowledge, to a full presentation of a case for the adoption of the Dewey Decimal Classification instead of Poole's own classification. Not only did they listen, but they approved—or led their informant to believe they had approved—the use of Dewey's system. When Poole was told by his subordinate of this decision, he caused its reversal, but the incident was not calculated to uphold his authority. On another occasion a staff member was informed directly of his appointment by the trustees as head of a newly established department. Although the appointment was in accordance with Poole's own recommendations, the staff member concerned was not aware of that fact. Again, the procedure followed had the effect of undermining Poole's authority. In addition, friends and even relatives of trustees were employed by the Newberry, a situation which seems to have been behind the assistant librarian's complaint of "this crowding in of favorites or friends of trustees." [6]

If the trustees took all too much interest in the daily affairs of the library, Poole took too little. He was extremely busy selecting books, planning for the permanent building, and attending to his many other responsibilities. Without a well-established organization, however, the functioning of the library was not wisely left to others to oversee. Some of the staff members had bitter comments to make about the failures in supervision, and even the friendly Evans commented privately: "There is more lack of system and more confusion here than I have been accustomed to have." [7]

Poole had always exercised supervision informally. The strong points of his staff relationships lay in his friendly interest in his assistants, his customary geniality, and the example of hard work which he set, together with his long years of experience that gave him ready answers to many problems that seemed new to his less seasoned assistants. When he worked closely with subordinates, he did well, but he was less effective when it was necessary for him to supervise at a distance. At the Chicago Public Library he had trained young men who, as the staff grew larger, took over the detailed supervisory responsibilities. At the Newberry the staff grew too fast, no young supervisor emerged to bridge the gap between Poole and the subordinate workers, and Poole waited too long to adopt a formal organization. Late in 1890, when the staff already included eighteen people, Poole finally did propose an organizational plan, which was put into effect in January, 1891. With improved order in the assignment of duties, the work of classifying and cataloging the books could proceed.

The classifying was done according to Poole's plan, shown in Table 1. It was hardly a classification at all, but merely a list of twenty-one subjects. They were not arranged in any logical sequence of relationships, nor were any detailed subdivisions provided. The details were to be furnished by individual classifiers. Poole claimed for his classification only that it was "simple and practicable." He had no use for elaborate schemes such as those devised by Dewey, Cutter, and others. He preferred his own, for "anybody who will see it in use can understand it, which is more than can be said of more complex systems." The notation was to be equally simple.

My shelf-marks mean simply *cases and the place of the book in the case.* I make no attempt to indicate the classification *by the shelf-mark,* in other words I do not mix up *classification* with *notation.* Classification of the books I make as minutely as I care to, and a *notation* of that classification by the shelf-marks, I have nothing to do with, for it is of no use to anybody. The catalogue gives the place of the book, and that is all that is wanted. The notation of some of these systems, in capitals, italics, lower-case letters, figures, greek [*sic*] letters, signs of the zodiac, punctuation marks, £, $,—all jumbled together to express some subdivision of classification—is very funny, and very absurd.

Poole's notation consisted of a letter to indicate a case or cases containing a broad subject, and a serial number to designate each book.[8]

As actually applied, the classification and the notation were somewhat more complicated than Poole's outline would indicate. Not only were the classifiers to provide for subject subdivisions, but they were also to plan the use of the serial numbers in such a way as to reserve blocks of numbers for each subclass. One purpose to be served by putting the responsibility in the hands of Dr. Williams was to ensure that the work would be done under the supervision of a man of broad education and culture. With a doctorate in history, Williams prided himself on a knowledge of that subject and of art and archeology as well. Poole would not have been apt to consider that there was a need for any better blueprint than that which he had provided. He had thought in 1876 that, with an outline of a classification and with a few explanatory examples of the subdivisions, "a librarian of intelligence, even if he has had little or no experience, ought to be able to arrange his books in a manner that shall be practically satisfactory." [9] Poole knew that Williams was a man of intelligence and some experience; surely there would be no difficulty. The result was a peculiar one. The classifiers were in need of guidance. As one of the most complete available schedules of subjects was Dewey's printed classification scheme, the classifiers used it extensively. The outcome was that, except for the notation and the arrangement of broad classes, a large part of the Poole-Newberry classification, particularly in natural science and useful arts, was taken from the very Dewey scheme of which Poole disapproved.

Poole seems not to have known that Dewey's plan was followed extensively, but he would have been unlikely to object if he had.

Table 1

POOLE CLASSIFICATION, THE NEWBERRY LIBRARY
1890–1895

A	Archeology
B	Bibliography
B1	Library Economy
C	Customs (Including Proverbs)
D	Documents
E	Education
F	Fine Arts
G	Geography
H (vol. 1)	Biography
H (vols. 2, 3)	History
I	Incunabula
La	Language
L	Literature
M	Music
N	Natural Sciences
O	Reference Books
P	Political Science
Ph	Philosophy
R	Religion
S	Serials
U	Useful Arts

Source: William Stetson Merrill, Report on Classification for the Newberry Library, January 19, 1895, typewritten MS in Newberry Library.

There was no reason why the classifiers should not obtain guidance from it, so long as they did not incorporate the fine details or use the mechanistic decimal notation. The important point was to avoid the complexities of the Dewey scheme—and for very practical reasons. Classification work under a broad scheme could be done quickly, whereas the precise subject determinations necessary under a close classification could be very time-consuming. It would be the matter of a moment to decide that a book was a work of natural history or even botany; it would take considerably longer to determine whether it concerned monocotyledons or dicotyledons or both, and, if both, which received the more important emphasis. Moreover, even after the books were classified, long and complicated call numbers made shelving and page work more difficult and expensive than was true with simple shelf marks.

Poole's classification was used during the rest of his regime. Even in that short time some of the classes became overcrowded. In order to piece out additional numbers, various expedients were used. Lower-case letters were added to numbers already used to provide an extra twenty-six spaces. A second expansive device was to treat the number already used as a class number, adding a second series of numbers as a subdivision of it. In the general reorganization under Poole's successor, the classification was abandoned. In its place was substituted the Cutter Expansive Classification with a specially devised notation. Poole's classification was probably discarded before it had outlived its usefulness, but it could hardly have lasted indefinitely at the Newberry any more than it did at the Chicago Public Library. Nor did Poole himself expect that it would. He had said in another connection: "It is not claimed that the writer's or any other plan will provide for indefinite expansion. The time will arrive when there must be an entire and radical re-arrangement." [10] Whatever its fate, the Poole classification was adopted and applied at the Newberry Library in 1890 and continued to be used until 1895.

At about the same time that the classification was adopted, work was begun on completing a card catalog of the collection. The library had always had a brief-entry catalog designed for staff use, but there had never been time or space to prepare a comprehensive public catalog. Poole seems, by this time, to have accepted the idea of a card catalog to be used by the patrons. In July, 1891, an assistant librarian was employed to serve as supervisor of the four department heads provided in the staff reorganization of the previous January. Charles Alexander Nelson was fifty-two years old when he came to the Newberry. He had recently been librarian of the Howard Memorial Library of New Orleans. Before that, he had prepared the notable catalog of the Astor Library. Presumably, his experience in cataloging was one of the prime reasons for his selection. On August 1, 1891, all additions to the library began to be recorded in a dictionary card catalog.

With a staff organization, a classification scheme, and a catalog under way, the necessary internal organization of the library was established. The basis for a change in the library's government was laid in July, 1891, with the passage of a new Illinois law authorizing the trustees of an endowed library to incorporate the institution. Blatchford and Bradley had concluded that the interests of the Newberry Library required a sizable board of trustees. Not only would the burdens of overseeing affairs be shared among the members of a larger body, but the future of the institution would be safer in the hands of a board than it was in the hands of only two men of advanced years. Even as it was, the new board had not yet taken office when, on March 1, 1892, Bradley died suddenly and unexpectedly. During the six weeks before the incorporation was completed, the continuity of control was precariously dependent upon the life of one man.

At last, on April 13, the new board was appointed. The trustees were a group whom Poole could have good reason to expect to influence. He had no thought that he had any control over the policies of the board as a matter of right: "Librarians must confess at the outset that the trustees are running the library; that the librarian is the servant of the trustees." [11] The librarian should have nothing to do with control of finances. "The trustees should have something to do, and that is the thing for them. . . . I have never seen a librarian yet who was a good financier. He should select and buy the books and attend to the general business." [12] On the other hand, it was, Poole thought, entirely proper that a librarian should seek to influence the board.

As librarian I have never claimed the right to attend meetings of the board of trustees, and yet I generally attended. They usually expected me to be present and give them information and suggestions. I give them no more advice than they ask for; and I think I have a good deal more influence over them for that reason.[13]

Several years earlier Poole had occasion to express his opinion of librarian-board relationships when Harry Lyman Koopman, later librarian of Brown University, considered seeking appointment at the public library of Grand Rapids, Michigan. A local businessman, Henry J. Carr, who was finally named to the position, wrote to Poole that he himself hesitated to accept because of dissension among the board members. Poole advised Koopman not to be deterred on that account:

If things have been going badly, and the Board has been split up I account for [it] in a large degree by the weakness and inefficiency of the librarian, and believe that these clouds would disappear if a competent librarian took the place. I have rather a taste for desperate cases. It gives a man a chance to show his mettle, and his services are appreciated. . . . If . . . they would elect you with a salary of $1200, I recommend you to accept, and go to work, make friends of the best material in the board and the public, use a good deal of judgment and worldly wisdom, and you will have the ground to yourself.[14]

In something of this fashion, Poole must have felt confident that he could obtain support from the majority of the Newberry's trustees. The board's membership gave him special grounds for confidence. The board was composed of Blatchford as president; George E. Adams, lawyer and recent Congressman from Illinois; Edward E. Ayer, a capitalist with large lumber interests: William Harrison Bradley, son of the late trustee and a U.S. consular representative in the years before and after 1892; Daniel Goodwin, lawyer; Franklin H. Head, manufacturer and banker; Edward S. Isham, law partner of Robert Todd Lincoln and the man who had represented the trustees in earlier litigation; General Alexander C. McClurg, bookseller and publisher; Franklin MacVeagh, wholesale grocer and banker, later Secretary of the Treasury under President Taft; General Walter C. Newberry, nephew of the donor and U.S. Congressman; Lambert Tree, lawyer and recent minister to Russia; Henry J. Willing, retired with a large fortune from Field, Leiter and Company; and John P. Wilson, senior partner of the legal firm of Wilson, Moore, and McIlvaine. Of these men, Blatchford at sixty-six was oldest and Wilson at forty-eight the youngest; the average of their ages was fifty-five. Ten of the thirteen trustees were members of the Chicago Literary Club, and another of them had been at one time. Both in the club and elsewhere, Poole had known most of these men over the years, and he could reasonably expect to be able to persuade them to follow his lead.

For the first months after the new board's appointment Poole's hopes seemed justified. Between April and the summer vacation in August orders for books were approved at twenty meetings of the Committee on Books, leading Poole to believe that a new day of free spending had begun. But, after this brief honeymoon period, the trustees began to scrutinize the orders more stringently than Blatchford and Bradley had done. As work on the new building began to require larger and larger sums of money, the trustees concluded that they must reduce expenses. Strict economy became a keynote of the library's operation. Poole's protests not only failed to change the trustees' opinion but helped to add to a growing feeling that his administration was not sufficiently economical. One of the complaints was that the staff was too large and included too many highly paid members.

In the middle of 1892 the staff consisted of about thirty people. At the head was Poole, whose duties included general oversight of the library, relations with the trustees, representation of the library to the public both in person and by correspondence, and, especially, selection of books. Nelson, the assistant librarian, was charged with responsibility for the administration of all departments and, in particular, with direction of the cataloging staff; he revised all cards, personally assigned subject headings, and made decisions on specific cataloging problems. Merrill, as head of the order and accession department, supervised a staff of ten, as well as handling such specific duties as recording packages received and certifying to the correctness of invoices. Allstrom, the library's general handyman, had special responsibility for unpacking shipments and for keeping the three collators supplied with books. Although Poole had said in 1876 that he no longer collated books, he made a distinction between the treatment of popular works and that given the more valuable and scholarly books bought for the Newberry. Martel kept the accession book. Two searchers, two file clerks, and an order copyist completed the staff of the department. The catalog department, under Nelson's special care, included eight catalogers and a "curator" who filed all cards in the catalogs. In the classification and reference department Evans, Frederick P. Noble, and Hanson assigned call numbers and recorded them in the shelf lists. This duty was divided by subject— Evans having Archeology, Customs, Education, Fine Arts, Language, and Natural Science; Noble having Geography, Literature, Philosophy, Religion, and Useful Arts; and Hanson having Bibliography, Biography and History, Library Economy, Music, Periodicals, Political Science, and Reference Books. Also under Evans were two men charged with the responsibility for the physical processing of new books, the preparation of volumes for the binders, and shelving in the main collections. The reading room staff consisted of Miss Mabel McIlvaine with two assistants for the daytime service. The reading room at night was supervised by various members of the staff who worked overtime for extra pay on a rotating basis. Although this work was voluntary, it was also necessary on a staff where one salary was as low as $312 a year. M. F. Morenius, curator of shelves and binding, added to his $720 annual salary by working 615 extra hours over and above the standard 42-hour week, thus earning an extra $205 during 1892. Some who were especially well educated were paid $1,200, others $1,000, $900, $720, and $600. Nelson received $3,000 and Poole $5,000. The median salary was $720. Although many of the salaries seem painfully low by later standards and were the subject of complaint, room and board at a first-class boarding house on Washington Park cost $8.00 a week. The twelve-room house rented for $75.00 a month, considered a very high rental for the time.

The organization plan, shown in Table 2, has some peculiarities which reflect the stage of the library's development and the special philosophy which governed the plans for the institution. The Newberry was still considered to be in its formative stages. The chief activities concerned the selection, acquisition, and processing of books. Poole gave his own principal attention to selection, and most of the staff were occupied with the other aspects of these functions. Only a few had, as their primary business, serving the patrons; even the desk attendants occupied their spare time in writing subject cards for the catalog. At the time, however, there was no need for more attendants, since the extensive division of

Table 2

ORGANIZATION CHART, NEWBERRY LIBRARY
August, 1892

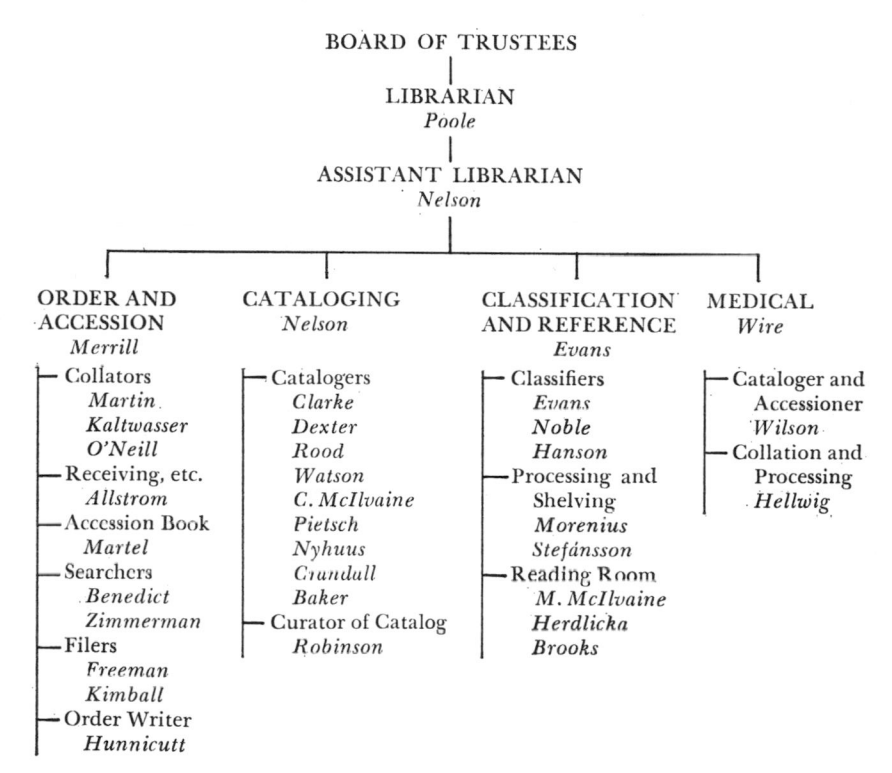

BOARD OF TRUSTEES
|
LIBRARIAN
Poole
|
ASSISTANT LIBRARIAN
Nelson

ORDER AND ACCESSION *Merrill*	CATALOGING *Nelson*	CLASSIFICATION AND REFERENCE *Evans*	MEDICAL *Wire*
├ Collators	├ Catalogers	├ Classifiers	├ Cataloger and
Martin	*Clarke*	*Evans*	Accessioner
Kaltwasser	*Dexter*	*Noble*	*Wilson*
O'Neill	*Rood*	*Hanson*	├ Collation and
├ Receiving, etc.	*Watson*	├ Processing and	Processing
Allstrom	*C. McIlvaine*	Shelving	*Hellwig*
├ Accession Book	*Pietsch*	*Morenius*	
Martel	*Nyhuus*	*Stefánsson*	
├ Searchers	*Crandall*	├ Reading Room	
Benedict	*Baker*	*M. McIlvaine*	
Zimmerman	├ Curator of Catalog	*Herdlicka*	
├ Filers	*Robinson*	*Brooks*	
Freeman			
Kimball			
├ Order Writer			
Hunnicutt			

Source: C. A. Nelson to the Committee on Administration, August 12, 1892, in Newberry Library.

the books into subject departments had not yet been made. The service functions performed by the classification and reference department would grow after the new building was occupied.

The term "reference" in the name of the classification and reference department seems to have meant more than the sense of "knowledgeable assistance to readers"; it included also the idea of the provision of means by which patrons could "refer" to the books in the collection. Although the reading room attendants in the Oak and State building did not have a thorough subject background, it was Poole's intention ultimately that the attendant in charge of each reading room should be well grounded in the subjects represented in that room's collections. The combination of classification work with reader service seems to reflect this conviction about the qualifications needed by the attendants.

During 1892 and 1893 the trustees took an increasingly close interest in all phases of the library's operation. Poole fought their reductions of book purchases, even twisting his instructions with literal and legalistic interpretations in order to escape their restrictions. But the trustees were not to be denied ultimately, and Poole, by forcing them to take a firm line on this matter, set a precedent by which the trustees treated him in a far more peremptory way than they had previously been willing to do.

Once they began this mode of dealing with him, they extended it to other matters. Initially, the trustees had been reluctant to express themselves unequivocally to Poole. Always a formidable antagonist, his person and his reputation seem to have overawed the trustees to an extent that, as individuals, they were most hesitant to state dissatisfactions explicitly. The result was a serious breakdown of communications between the board and its librarian. Finally, in March, 1893, one of the trustees got up his courage to express himself directly to Poole. Late in the month Franklin MacVeagh was in Asheville, North Carolina; perhaps the distance from Chicago allowed him to see in clear perspective how badly things were going at the Newberry. Emboldened by long years of friendship, he wrote Poole a letter whose warning the librarian should have taken to heart:

> Will you take a word from me in the spirit in which it is spoken? You and I have been friends for a good many years—and I hope you will believe that I am now giving you a sincere proof of my friendship, in giving you a hint of what I believe the growing attitude of the Newberry trustees will be because it is already the growing attitude of the Committee on the Administration of the Library. . . .

The fact is then that there exists a strong disapproval—in the Committee especially—of the cost of the Administration; and a profound doubt of the efficiency of the organization. . . . The sentiment is growing that the responsibility for the reform of the Administration rests upon you. Indeed this view, I confess, seems to me eminently just; but I have come to believe that it has not occurred to your mind, and therefore I put you up to it [*sic*]. Depend upon it, Doctor, you will sooner or later be considered wholly responsible for that departments [*sic*] expenses and efficiency. Everything grows and tends in that direction. Hence this letter.

To reconstruct the Administration seems necessary to the Committee, I think—indeed am sure. And my hint to you is to *go at it yourself* and propose a plan. It will probably involve more of the oversight of the work of the library by yourself—and the savings of other considerable salaries. . . . I know that until a year ago you were probably relieved of all the responsibilities; but under the present regime the feeling is growing that *the reform should emanate from the head of the Library.*

MacVeagh's letter might have been enough to have alerted some men, but it was not sufficient to make Poole realize the seriousness of the situation. Poole did recommend some changes, but they were not enough to achieve the *"very large* reductions" which MacVeagh said were necessary. The letter remained as only an early outcropping of difficulties which were to deepen during the rest of the year. The Committee on Administration soon took drastic action itself.[15]

Despite the wish to economize on staff, the trustees were also concerned at the slowness of cataloging. Although every book in the library was listed in the official catalog or in special lists which came with large collections bought *en bloc,* the dictionary catalog was not complete. In May the Committee on Administration called in Nelson to report on the state of the work. They evidently considered the performance unsatisfactory; at least, on the same day his report was received, the committee voted to abolish his position at the end of the current year of service, ostensibly to economize on staff salaries.

In retrospect, the decision seems a mistake. Among Nelson's professional colleagues his reputation was so good that he was promptly employed at Columbia College as assistant librarian, a position in which he completed his career. It is impossible to determine whether the amount of cataloging arrearage was reasonable or not. It is always difficult for laymen to understand that cataloging takes time and that a certain amount of backlog is a necessity to efficient operation of a cataloging department. In any case, card production dropped after Nelson's departure. It is clear that he was far from useless to the library, and the need for responsible assistance was especially acute in the middle of 1893.

Nelson's departure put the responsibility for close supervision of the staff back into Poole's hands. A less opportune time for such a change could hardly have been chosen. Poole had been employed at the Newberry because he had a national—indeed a world-wide—reputation as a librarian and as a man of affairs in the realm of scholarship. This position involved regular responsibilities which the original trustees recognized in granting him time and expense allowances to attend meetings of the American Library Association and at least the time to attend the American Historical Association conventions. And, in 1893, the year of the city's Columbian Exposition, a man in his position was obliged to participate in that great enterprise. When Nelson's services were abruptly cut off, Poole was in the midst of the most pressing kind of duties. Ever since the first of the year, he had been engaged in extensive correspondence arranging for a star-studded group of historians to address the World's Historical Congress. He himself was chairman of the Committee on Arrangements, and, when the congress opened, he took the chair initially. The success of the meeting was largely attributed to the arrangements which he had made.

The Historical Congress was only the most important of Poole's responsibilities at the Exposition. He also attended and spoke at the Chicago conference of the American Library Association. He spoke twice before the Chicago Library Club and once before the Chicago Literary Club. And he delivered the Phi Beta Kappa address at Northwestern University. This address, "The University Library and the University Curriculum," was a kind of valedictory. He sought to show that

the study of Bibliography and of the scientific methods of using books should have an assured place in the University Curriculum; that a

Officers of the American Historical Association, December 30, 1889.
Left to right: Poole, Justin Winsor, Charles Kendall Adams, Herbert B. Adams, George Bancroft, Clarence W. Bowen, John Jay, Andrew D. White

wise and professional bibliographer should be a member of the faculty and have a part in training all the students; that the Library should be his class room, and that all who go forth into the world as graduates should have such an intelligent and practical knowledge of books as will aid them in their studies through life, and the use of books be to them a perpetual delight and refreshment. Books are wiser than any professor and all the faculty; and they can be made to give up much of their wisdom to the student who knows where to go for it, and how to extract it.

I do not mean that the university student should learn the contents of the most useful books; but I do mean that he should know of their existence, what they treat of, and what they will do for him. . . . He should know the standard writers on a large variety of subjects. He should be familiar with the best method by which the original investigation of any topic may be carried on. When he has found it, he appreciates, perhaps for the first time, what books are for, and how to use them. He finds himself a professional literary or scientific worker, and that books are the tools of his profession. . . . This facile proficiency does not come by intuition, nor from the clouds. Where else is it to be taught, if not in the college or university? [16]

Poole had discussed his conceptions of the proper uses of books during the previous year at two successive meetings of the Chicago Library Club:

There is a common opinion that people who read a good deal know a good deal. This may be true or may not be true, for it all depends on the effects of the reading. I call that reading beneficial which makes us think, sets us to do our own thinking. . . .
I am constantly asked, "What shall I read?" My answer is, "Read what interests you. Baseball, fishing, Italy, Switzerland, witchcraft, philosophy, or what not. Pick out something you are interested in, and master it completely."

It was not necessary, he thought, to read every book "from title page to index." A person should be able to read a book on a familiar subject in a single evening.

A person ought to read with a definite subject in his serious reading. Every one should have a special subject, and examine it in all its varied relations. . . . How shall a person "read"? I think a person should read as if he was to write upon that subject. He should keep this in view, and I think no one has read a book properly unless he has put himself in position to write about it. . . . I read with a block of paper at hand. . . . I make over the thought of the author into my own language, and this I retain, but not the literal language of the author.

. . . This practice trains us in observing the leading points, in clear thinking, and in concise modes of expression.[17]

Addressing local learned clubs and planning and participating in national conferences were aspects of Poole's life which had been taken into account at the time of his appointment and which had always been a part of his professional life. The Newberry's trustees, while mindful of the work of the library, might have been wiser to have weighed these responsibilities, which reflected credit on the institution, before precipitously divesting their librarian of his chief assistant.

Although it is possible that the abolition of the position was simply a maneuver to get rid of Nelson, it appears that the trustees did indeed intend that Poole take over the detailed supervisory duties himself. If so, they changed their minds within a short time. By July they were beginning a search for a new assistant librarian. By September, as it had proved impossible to find a man at the salary they proposed to pay, they began to think in terms of appointing a man with top qualifications at a larger salary. They offered Frederick M. Crunden of the St. Louis Public Library an appointment as director of the library, apparently with the intention of leaving Poole as librarian. After Crunden refused the appointment and they were unable to find another man to take a subordinate position at the salary they were willing to pay, they finally decided to clear the way by reducing Poole's responsibilities, authority, and salary.

The trustees had as their ultimate responsibility the interests of the institution. Even if they had recognized more fully than they seem to have done the inescapable nature of many of Poole's outside activities, especially during the hectic year of 1893, they could not forever have ignored what was, in their judgment, his inadequate administration of the library. In November the Committee on Administration recommended that Poole be made consulting librarian at half salary. His duties were "to be advisory in their nature and to relate more particularly to the purchase of books and to the scope and lines of development of the library." [18] The full board adopted the report and authorized the committee to undertake negotiations with Poole on the matter, adding only that his salary would remain unchanged for the first year.

The board's action was not lacking in generosity, nor, especially in light of the general view of the time concerning the obligations of employer to employee, was it unjustified. It seems clear that Poole had kept aloof from daily affairs to a greater extent than was wise. His occupation with building plans, book selection, and outside scholarly activities were not well advised to the extent that they kept him from seeing to the smooth running of the library's day-to-day activities. It is an unfortunate but perhaps necessary characteristic of librarianship that the head of a library can never pick out and concentrate upon one aspect of his library's operation to the neglect of the whole. In this respect the librarian differs from the practitioners of many other professions. For example, a professor who has taught for many years may, by virtue of his writing and outside lecturing, build up a reputation which enables him, in effect, to neglect the teaching which lies at the core of his duties. The librarian, by contrast, is the head of an operating agency, and he must see that it runs efficiently during the whole of his tenure. If he does not, no other accomplishment in writing, lecturing, book selection, building plans, or any other activity will save his position or, at the least, his untarnished reputation. The history of librarianship in the United States is filled with sad stories of librarians who, having made great contributions and reputations, relaxed their vigilance over the whole in order to pursue one aspect which particularly appealed to them or in which they were particularly gifted. So it was with Poole, even though the visible evidences of his work were so clear—among them a substantial book collection and an impressive new building, occupied just in the midst of these deliberations over his future. On November 15, 1893, the work of moving began, and he soon had the great satisfaction of seeing the books which he had bought placed in the building which he had planned.

The pleasure of seeing the fruit of seven years of work was mingled with the shock of the trustees' decision. He had been aware of dissatisfaction with specific problems, but even Mac-

Veagh's letter does not seem to have given him any realization that the displeasure ran so deep. He had relinquished his position at the public library to undertake the new task of developing a great research institution. Now, just as his work was coming to fruition, the trustees proposed to take it from his hands. He set himself to win back their confidence by the vigor with which he would regain satisfactory control of the library's administration. Early in January the board, having received a refusal from another prospective candidate, decided to delay any further effort to find a new man until after the new committees were appointed in April. By that time, however, it was no longer a matter of finding a man to displace Poole but of finding one to succeed him.

Poole remained at the Newberry during the early part of 1894. He continued to write cheerful letters. He wrote a review for *The Dial.* When a young Boston lad asked for his autograph, he replied with a variant quotation from his Phi Beta Kappa address: "Books are wiser than any university professor and all the faculty, and can be made to give up much of their wisdom to the student who knows where to go for it, and how to extract it." [19] He still had his old dry wit. He wrote to the librarian of the Massachusetts Historical Society:

Last Saturday another batch of old newspapers was offered me for sale, and the most precious one was claimed to be another much worn copy of this *Ulster Co. Gazette!* On the first page (left upper margin), was printed "*Copyright secured.*" The person who brought the batch asked for an offer for the lot. I offered ten cents, and the person vanished.[20]

Poole had met criticism and adversity before. And this time, too, he kept his courage and his pride. He remained cheerful on the surface. But something—and the likelihood is that the blow of the trustees' decision played its part—began to tell on him. He developed severe headaches and insomnia, and then he contracted a mild case of the grippe. For a time he came to the library for a part of each day, but then he stayed close to home. After he had suffered several damaging falls, his illness and weakness increased; finally, he went into a coma. Early on the morning of March 1, 1894, he died.

The funeral, preceded by private services at the house, was held on Saturday, March 3, in the First Congregational Church of Evanston; the minister, Dr. J. F. Loba, was assisted by Poole's Yale classmate, Franklin W. Fisk, president of the Chicago Theological Seminary. It is said to have been one of the largest funerals held in Evanston in years. The active pallbearers were three employees from the Newberry and three from the public library. The honorary pallbearers were President Rogers and Professor Daniel Bonbright of Northwestern University, President Harper of the University of Chicago, Frederick Hild of the public library, Norman L. Williams, former public library board member and Crerar trustee, Henry J. Willing, the only representative of the Newberry's board, and eight other distinguished citizens. The funeral sermon was based on the text, "Know ye not that there is a prince and a great man fallen this day in Israel?" The body was taken East for burial in the family lot in Peabody.

XIV. Portrait of a Librarian

William Frederick Poole's forty-seven years as a librarian epitomized the development of American librarianship during the nineteenth century. When he began his service in social libraries, no free, publicly supported institutions existed. After the Civil War, when public libraries were springing up all over the country, he joined the new movement. As head of two of the most important public libraries of the nation and as adviser to others, he was a leader in making the institution an established part of American society. Finally, he turned to the research institution that could serve scholars, who were increasing in number and in the formality of their training and employment.

Achievements as the executive head of libraries formed the framework of Poole's professional life, but they were only a part of his accomplishments. Creation of the periodical index that made his name well known to his own and later generations was important not only as the inauguration of a new bibliographical form but also as a demonstration of remarkable energy and devotion to scholarship. The use of cooperative means to produce the great third edition proved the feasibility of the method and made the *Index* a forerunner of a number of similar cooperative ventures. In line with the literary orientation of the *Index,* Poole's employment of his leisure time in writing reviews and historical articles further demonstrated the dedication to learning so often found among nineteenth-century leaders. His own high place in their ranks was attested by his election as president of the American Historical Association.

Poole's avocational writing enriched his professional life, but libraries were the center of his career. His contributions were made through his services as head of his own libraries, as active member and president of the American Library Association, and as frequent adviser to others. Serving as mentor of young librarians, Poole played a part in the early careers of an impressive array of distinguished librarians, many of whom, significantly, achieved their chief reputations as bibliographers rather than as technicians and administrators.

Poole's own inclination toward the bibliographical side of librarianship may have been one factor behind difficulties that, on several occasions, seem to reflect certain deficiencies in his capacity as an administrator of library staffs. Even in that respect, however, his successes far outweigh the failures. Another area of librarianship that seems deficient was Poole's system and grasp of the technicalities of cataloging and classification. It is not altogether sure, however, that his positions on these matters were without merit. In the long perspective of American library experience, it is to be questioned whether the turn to close and exact rules and procedures did not bring, along with the apparent benefits, a rigidity and an elaborateness that cost more than the advantages were worth. Flexibility and constant adjustment to changing and varying needs, which Poole advocated, might have been wisely bought at the cost of exactness and precision.

The flexibility of Poole's mind kept his viewpoint fresh and vigorous. One who was initiated to librarianship under his direction said of him: "Perhaps only once since in the library world, in the person of John Cotton Dana, have [I] met what seemed to me as free, original and creative a mind." [1] In no other area of Poole's interest was his originality better exemplified than in his proposals in the field of library architecture and organization. The insistence upon functional design was fresh and modern at a time when even among architects such an approach was considered new and heretical. He recognized early that new structural materials made possible broad spans of open space in reading rooms. Although he was only one of many librarians who condemned traditional library architecture, he stood almost alone in his advocacy of low-ceilinged, flexible space as contrasted with the architectural rigidity imposed by the book stack. As a corollary to Poole's ideas for buildings, he stood for subject departmentalization as the plan of service best adapted to the needs of library patrons. The twin proposals, long neglected by librarianship, came to form a keynote of later library practice.

Specific ideas, administrative achievements, and training of young librarians were important among Poole's contributions, but his contemporaries placed high on the list his leadership in making librarianship a recognized profession. In the cities he served he took a prominent and respected position. His own self-respect, scholarship, and vigor made his fellow citizens recognize him as a man of importance in the community. He dealt with politicians, businessmen, scholars, and professional people alike on terms of equality. He understood the legitimacy of the interest in the public library taken by individuals and groups. He did not shrink from public criticism, but he did not fear to answer it vigorously if he thought it worthwhile to do so. By free participation in the affairs of the community he brought the library and the figure of the librarian into the public consciousness as a part of daily life. He himself was well known, and, by that fact, he created an image of the librarian as something more than a shy, retiring keeper of books.

Poole was able to project a picture of the librarian as a person of importance because he was himself a vigorous, positive, and forthright man. His warmth and humor, his devotion to his profession, his standing as a scholar, and his fearless entry into the public arena made him a figure of strength wherever he went. Whatever his faults, they were dwarfed by his force and pride, his self-respect and vigor, his competence and knowledge, and, above all, by his warmth and strength as a man. Those who follow him in the profession he loved may learn much from his career and may take pride in succeeding such a leader.

Notes

I: The Years of Preparation

1. Yale College, Class of 1846, *Record of the Class* (New Haven, The Class, 1871), p. 4.
2. Poole, *The University Library*, p. 50.
3. American Library Association, "The Proceedings [of the Conference]," *Library Journal*, XVI (1891), C88. Hereafter cited as ALA, "Proceedings."
4. Poole to Addison Van Name, March 6, 1878, in Yale University Library.
5. ALA, "Proceedings," *Library Journal*, I (1876–77), 116.
6. "Editors' Table," *Yale Literary Magazine*, XII (1846–47), 192.
7. Poole, *Index* (1882), p. iii.
8. Poole, *Index* (1853), p. v.
9. Poole, *Index* (1882), p. iii.
10. Autograph book of Washington Murray, July 2, 1849, in Yale University Library.
11. *Ibid.*
12. Poole to Edward W. Herrick, February 28, 1852, in Yale University Library.

II: The Start of a Career, 1852–1856

1. Mercantile Library Association, *Annual Report*, 1856, pp. 29–31.
2. *Ibid.*, 1853, pp. 4–5.
3. *Ibid.*, 1853, pp. 14–15.
4. Poole, "Address of the President," *Library Journal*, XI (1886), 200.
5. New York *Times*, December 17, 1853.
6. Cutter, "Library Catalogues," in U.S. Bureau of Education, *Public Libraries in the United States*, p. 534.
7. *Ibid.*, p. 534.
8. Mercantile Library Association, *Annual Report*, 1855, p. 23.
9. Secretary's records, Mercantile Library Association, in Boston University Library. I am indebted to Macy Margolis for information from these files.
10. Mercantile Library Association, *Annual Report*, 1856, pp. 35–36.

III: The Boston Athenaeum, 1856–1868

1. Jewett, *Notices of Public Libraries*, p. 22.
2. Poole to Library Committee, June 2, 1856, in Boston Athenaeum.

3. Boston Athenaeum, *The Athenaeum Centenary*, p. 41
4. William I. Fletcher, "Some Recollections of the Boston Athenaeum, 1861–1866," *Library Journal*, XXXIX (1914), 582.
5. *Ibid.*, p. 582.
6. R. W. Hooper to H. B. Rogers, April 18, 1857, in Boston Athenaeum.
7. Letterbook copy, Poole to James L. Donaldson, October 21, 1865, in Boston Athenaeum.
8. Letterbook copy, Poole to Fitch Poole, October 20, 1865, in Boston Athenaeum.
9. "Poole's Index Committee—Third Report," *Library Journal*, I (1876–77), 324.
10. Committee of Inquiry into the Index Catalogue of the Library to the Trustees, November 16, 1868, in Boston Athenaeum.
11. Charles A. Cutter to unidentified member of the Trustees, November 21, 1868, in Boston Athenaeum.
12. Fletcher, "Some Recollections of the Boston Athenaeum, 1861–1866," *Library Journal*, XXXIX (1914), 581.
13. Poole to F. E. Parker, February 15, 1868, in Boston Athenaeum.
14. Roden, "The Boston Years of Dr. W. F. Poole," in Bishop and Keogh, *Essays*, pp. 388–94.
15. Library Committee to the Trustees, undated report for the year 1868, in Boston Athenaeum.

IV: Library Expert, 1869 and Later

1. Boston *Directory*, 1869.
2. Poole to Winsor, January 12, 1871, in Boston Public Library.
3. Buffalo, Young Men's Association, *Thirty-fourth Annual Report of the Executive Committee* (Buffalo, The Association, 1870), pp. 8–9.
4. Quoted phrases from a letter from William Stetson Merrill to the author.
5. Josephus N. Larned, at Poole memorial meeting, ALA, "Proceedings," *Library Journal*, XIX (1894), C169.
6. Poole to Daniel Coit Gilman, May 21, 1870, in The Johns Hopkins University Library.
7. Poole to Winsor, October 4, 1871, in Boston Public Library.
8. Cincinnati Public Library, *Annual Report*, 1870–71, p. 23.

V: Cincinnati Public Library, 1869–1873

1. Cincinnati Public Library, *Annual Report*, 1870–71, p. 8.
2. Poole to Charles Evans, June 29, 1872, in Evans Papers.
3. Cincinnati Public Library, *Annual Report*, 1871–72, pp. 20–21.
4. Letterbook copies, Poole to H. B. Lane, February 10, 1871, May 28, 1872, and April 26, 1873, in Cincinnati Public Library.
5. ALA, "Proceedings," *Library Journal*, I (1876–77), 110.
6. Cincinnati Public Library, *Annual Report*, 1871–72, p. 34.

7. *Ibid.*, pp. 6–7.
8. *Volksblatt,* November 1, 1873.
9. Poole to Charles Evans, November 27, 1872, in Evans Papers.
10. Cincinnati Public Library, *Annual Report,* 1898–99, p. 36.

VI: Chicago Public Library, 1874–1879

1. Spencer, *The Chicago Public Library.*
2. Poole, "The Organization and Management of Public Libraries," pp. 477–78.
3. Poole to Rutherford B. Hayes, February 10, 1874, in Rutherford B. Hayes Library.
4. Poole, "The Organization and Management of Public Libraries," p. 484.
5. *Ibid.*, p. 481.
6. *Ibid.*, p. 489.
7. ALA, "Proceedings," *Library Journal,* I (1876–77), 134.
8. Quoted by Otis H. Robinson, "College Library Administration," in U.S. Bureau of Education, *Public Libraries in the United States,* p. 512.
9. Poole, "The Organization and Management of Public Libraries," p. 490.
10. *Ibid.*, p. 498.
11. Poole to Charles Evans, June 14, 1874, in Evans Papers.
12. Poole, "The Organization and Management of Public Libraries," pp. 492–94.
13. I am indebted to Mrs. Roberta B. Sutton of the Chicago Public Library for a detailed description of the 1874 finding list.
14. Poole to Winsor, August 2, 1872, in Boston Public Library.
15. Poole, "The Organization and Management of Public Libraries," p. 498.
16. Chicago Public Library, *Annual Report,* 1873–74, p. 22.
17. *Ibid.*, p. 26.
18. Poole to Winsor, September 6, 1875, in Boston Public Library.
19. Chicago Public Library, *Annual Report,* 1873–74, pp. 32–33.
20. Poole to Rutherford B. Hayes, February 10, 1874, in Rutherford B. Hayes Library.
21. Poole to Winsor, July 3, 1872, in Boston Public Library.
22. Poole to Charles Evans, August 24, 1872, in Evans Papers.
23. Poole to Charles Evans, August 26, 1874, in Evans Papers.
24. Poole to Edmund M. Barton, March 19, 1891, in American Antiquarian Society.
25. *The Owl,* I–II, No. 3 (October, 1874–March, 1876).
26. ALA, "Proceedings," *Library Journal,* II (1877–78), p. 36.
27. Gookin, *The Chicago Literary Club,* p. 6.
28. Quoted, *ibid.*, p. 11.
29. *Ibid.*, pp. 11–12.
30. *Ibid.*, p. 12.
31. Poole to Winsor, July 3, 1872, in Boston Public Library.
32. Poole, "Some Popular Objections to Public Libraries," *Library Journal,* I (1876–77), 50.

33. Poole, "The Organization and Management of Public Libraries," p. 478.
34. Poole, "State Legislation in the Matter of Libraries," *Library Journal,* II (1877–78), 12.
35. Chicago Public Library, *Annual Report,* 1874–75, p. 17.
36. Poole, "Public Libraries of Chicago," in U.S. Bureau of Education, *Public Libraries in the United States,* p. 897.
37. Chicago Public Library, *Annual Report,* 1876–77, p. 34.

VII: The American Library Association

1. Poole to Winsor, November 17, 1875, in Boston Public Library.
2. Quoted in Poole to Dewey, December 28, 1883, in Columbia University Libraries.
3. Poole to Winsor, May 27 and May 31, 1876, in Boston Public Library.
4. Poole to Dewey, December 28, 1883, in Columbia University Libraries.
5. William E. Foster, "Five Men of '76," American Library Association, *Bulletin,* XX (1926), 314–15.
6. ALA, "Proceedings," *Library Journal,* II (1877–78), 36.
7. Dewey, at Poole memorial meeting, ALA, "Proceedings," *Library Journal,* XIX (1894), C169.
8. Poole to Charles Evans, May 19, 1874, in Evans Papers.
9. Editorial, *Library Journal,* II (1877–78), 14.
10. ALA, "Proceedings," *Library Journal,* II (1877–78), 29.
11. ALA, "Proceedings," *Library Journal,* XIV (1889), 284–85.
12. ALA, "Proceedings," *Library Journal,* X (1885), 309.
13. Poole to Dewey, December 28, 1883, in Columbia University Libraries.
14. Poole, "Address of the President," *Library Journal,* XI (1886), 202.
15. Poole to Winsor, January 30, 1882, in Massachusetts Historical Society.
16. Ernest C. Richardson, "Why Librarians Know," *Library Journal,* XI (1886), 204.
17. Poole to Winsor, May 22, 1892, in Massachusetts Historical Society.

VIII: Poole's Index

1. "Poole's Index Committee—Second Report," *Library Journal,* I (1876–77), 287.
2. Poole, "The Plan of the New 'Poole's Index,'" *Library Journal,* III (1878), 110.
3. Otis H. Robinson, *et al.,* "Cooperative College Cataloguing," *Library Journal,* I (1876–77), 436.
4. ALA, "Proceedings," *Library Journal,* II (1877–78), 18.
5. ALA, "Proceedings," *Library Journal,* VIII (1883), 265.
6. *Ibid.,* p. 261.
7. Poole to Winsor, February 11, 1878, in Harvard University Library.
8. Poole to Edmund M. Barton, March 15, 1878, in American Antiquarian Society.
9. Poole to Addison Van Name, March 6, 1878, in Yale University Library.

Notes

10. Poole to Addison Van Name, March 28, 1878, in Yale University Library.
11. *Ibid.*
12. Poole to N. H. Morison, December 30, 1882, in Peabody Institute of Baltimore.
13. Poole, "The Index Symposium and Its Moral," *Library Journal*, III (1878), 178, 185.
14. Poole to Winsor, January 16, 1882, in Massachusetts Historical Society.
15. Poole to Benjamin Holt Ticknor, April 6, 1882, in Library of Congress.
16. "Bibliografy," *Library Journal*, VII (1882), 296; "Poole's New Index," *Science*, I (1883), 68.
17. "American Literature," *Saturday Review*, LV (January–June, 1883), 127.
18. "Poole's Index," *Nation*, XXXVI (January–June, 1883), 63–64; "An Index to Periodical Literature," *Athenaeum*, January–June, 1883, 118–19; William E. A. Axon, "An Index to Periodical Literature," *Academy*, XXIII (January–June, 1883), 127–28.
19. Poole to Winsor, January 25, 1883, in Massachusetts Historical Society.
20. Poole, "Supplements to Poole's Index," *Library Journal*, VIII (1883), 194.
21. ALA, "Proceedings," *Library Journal*, X (1885), 318.
22. "Editorial," *Library Journal*, XIII (1888), 276.

IX: Later Years at the Chicago Public Library, 1879–1886

1. Chicago Public Library, *Annual Report*, 1873–74, p. 34.
2. Chicago Public Library, *Annual Report*, 1881–82, p. 23.
3. George E. Wire, at Poole memorial meeting, ALA, "Proceedings," *Library Journal*, XIX (1894), C168.
4. Chicago Public Library, *Annual Report*, 1881–82, p. 23.
5. Poole to Dewey, July 14, 1883, in Columbia University Libraries.
6. *The Inter-Ocean*, February 13, 1883, quoted in *Library Journal*, VIII (1883), 52.
7. ALA, "Proceedings," *Library Journal*, VIII (1883), 281.
8. Evanston *Index*, August 7, 1880.
9. Chicago Public Library, *Annual Report*, 1884–85, p. 24.
10. Chicago *Times*, May 24, 1879, quoted in *Library Journal*, IV (1879), 209.
11. Poole to Winsor, May 26, 1879, in Harvard University Library.

X: Association President and Library Leader, 1886–1887

1. Chicago Public Library, *Annual Report*, 1885–86, p. 27.
2. Edward G. Mason, quoted in Gookin, *The Chicago Literary Club*, p. 159.
3. Chicago Public Library, *Proceedings of the Board*, 1886–88, p. 135.
4. *Ibid.*, p. 147.
5. Chicago *Tribune*, July 16, 1887.
6. Poole to Dewey, July 19, 1887, in Columbia University Libraries.
7. Charles Evans to Poole, July 28, 1887, in Newberry Library.
8. "Newberry Library," *Athenaeum*, July–December, 1887, 213.

9. Poole to Samuel Austin Allibone, August 2, 1887, in New York Public Library.
10. Autograph book of Washington Murray, July 2, 1849, in Yale University Library.
11. Poole, "Address of the President," *Library Journal,* XII (1887), 311–20.

XI: Newberry Library: Acquiring a Collection

1. Poole to Charles Evans, April 23, 1891, in Evans Papers.
2. Letterbook copy, Poole to Joseph C. Rowell, January 8, 1892, in Newberry Library.
3. Letterbook copy, Poole to B. F. Stevens, September 16, 1887, in Newberry Library.
4. Poole to Edmund M. Barton, April 22, 1893, in American Antiquarian Society.
5. Letterbook copy, Poole to H. C. Potter, July 27, 1888, in Newberry Library.
6. Letterbook copy, Poole to F. C. Würtele, January 4, 1888, in Newberry Library.
7. Poole to Edmund M. Barton, September 23, 1887, in American Antiquarian Society.
8. Letterbook copy, Poole to Henry Probasco, December 19, 1889, in Newberry Library.
9. Letterbook copy, Poole to Henry Probasco, August 16, 1889, in Newberry Library.
10. Quoted in Stanley Pargellis, "The Building of a Library," *Newberry Library Bulletin,* No. 1 (November, 1944), 6.
11. Newberry Library, *Annual Report,* 1889, p. 6.
12. Poole to Committee on Books, October 31, 1892, in Newberry Library.
13. Poole to Board of Trustees, March 20, 1893, in Newberry Library.
14. Poole to Committee on Books, October 31, 1892, in Newberry Library.

XII: Newberry Library: Planning a Building

1. Poole, "Report on Library Architecture," *Library Journal,* VII (1882), 136.
2. Poole, "The Construction of Library Buildings," *Library Journal,* VI (1881), 73.
3. Poole, "Small Library Buildings," *Library Journal,* X (1885), 251.
4. Poole to Charles Evans, April 23, 1891, in Evans Papers.
5. Charles Evans to Poole, October 14, 1890, in Newberry Library.
6. Poole, "Remarks at the Publishers' and Booksellers' Dinner," *Library Journal,* XV (1890), C165–66.
7. Robert E. Maizell, "The Subject-Departmentalized Public Library," *College and Research Libraries,* XII (1951), 255–60.
8. Poole, "The Construction of Library Buildings," *Library Journal,* VI (1881), 73.
9. *Ibid.,* p. 70.

10. Poole, *Remarks on Library Construction*, p. 23.
11. ALA, "Proceedings," *Library Journal*, XVI (1891), C101.
12. Chicago *Tribune*, December 29, 1889, quoted in *Library Journal*, XV (1890), 48–50.
13. Poole to Herbert B. Adams, January 13, 1890, in The Johns Hopkins University Library.
14. ALA, "Proceedings," *Library Journal*, XV (1890), C107.
15. Poole to Herbert B. Adams, December 16, 1893, and January 12, 1894, in The Johns Hopkins University Library.

XIII: Newberry Library: Administering a Library, 1887–1894

1. Poole to George Watson Cole, March 28, 1888, in American Antiquarian Society.
2. Letterbook copy, Poole to N. C. Ricker, May 13, 1889, in Newberry Library.
3. Poole to Committee on Books, October 31, 1892, in Newberry Library.
4. Poole, in "Being a Librarian [Symposium]" *Library Journal*, XV (1890), 202.
5. Poole to Committee on Administration, October 14, 1892, in Newberry Library.
6. ALA, "Proceedings," *Library Journal*, XVIII (1893), C38.
7. Charles Evans to Lena Evans, July 19, 1892, in Evans Papers.
8. Letterbook copy, Poole to Henry Matson, January 30, 1885, in Chicago Public Library.
9. Poole, "The Organization and Management of Public Libraries," p. 493.
10. *Ibid.*, p. 494.
11. ALA, "Proceedings," *Library Journal*, XVIII (1893), C64.
12. *Ibid.*, p. C63.
13. *Ibid.*, p. C64.
14. Poole to Harry Lyman Koopman, December 22, 1885, in Brown University Library.
15. Franklin MacVeagh to Poole, March 27, 1893, in Newberry Library.
16. Poole, *The University Library*, pp. 3–6.
17. "Chicago Library Club," *Library Journal*, XVII (1892), 101, 132–33.
18. Minutes of Committee on Administration, November 16, 1893, in Newberry Library.
19. Poole to Howes Norris, Jr., January 15, 1894, in possession of the author.
20. Poole to Samuel A. Green, January 24, 1894, in Massachusetts Historical Society.

XIV: Portrait of a Librarian

1. Marilla Waite Freeman to author, August, 1953.

Selected Bibliography

General Note

Basic printed sources for this study are the *Library Journal* from 1876 to 1894 and the annual reports of the Mercantile Library Association of Boston, the Cincinnati Public Library, the Chicago Public Library, and the Newberry Library. The last three of these institutions possess scrapbooks containing comprehensive collections of newspaper clippings for the period of Poole's regime. These three libraries, and the Boston Athenaeum as well, have Poole's letterbooks recording a part of his official correspondence. Official records of various kinds, usually including minutes of meetings of library committees and governing boards, are available for the Society of the Brothers in Unity, the Mercantile Library Association of Boston, the Boston Athenaeum, the Bronson Library of Waterbury, Connecticut, the Grosvenor Library, the Cincinnati Public Library, the Chicago Public Library, and the Newberry Library. The only large body of incoming correspondence that has been preserved is the Poole Papers at the Newberry Library. The manuscript depositories in which Poole's letters have been found are listed in the Preface.

Poole's Writings

Poole's writings may be identified through the following publications:

Chicago Literary Club. *In Memoriam William Frederick Poole*. Chicago, The Club, 1894.
Library Journal; General Index to Vols. I–XXII. New York, The Journal, 1898.
Newberry Library. Board of Trustees. *Memorial Sketch of Dr. William Frederick Poole*. Chicago, The Library, 1895.

Book reviews by Poole appeared in Boston newspapers during the time of his residence there, but their identification would be difficult if not impossible. One article not listed in the sources above is "Who Owns Spot Pond?" which appeared in the Malden *Messenger,* April 3, 1869. Although the subject matter is of localized interest, the article is of some importance as an example of Poole's historical writing.

Printed Materials

Bagg, Lyman Hotchkiss. *Four Years at Yale.* New Haven, Charles C. Chatfield, 1871.

Borome, Joseph A. *Charles Coffin Jewett.* Chicago, American Library Association, 1951.

Boston Athenaeum. *The Athenaeum Centenary; the Influence and History of the Boston Athenaeum from 1807 to 1907.* Boston, The Athenaeum, 1907.

Chicago Literary Club. *In Memoriam William Frederick Poole.* Chicago, The Club, 1894.

Cincinnati Public Library. *Annual Report of the Board of Trustees for the Year Ending June 30, 1899.* Cincinnati, The Library, 1899.

Decrow, W. E. *Yale and "The City of Elms."* Boston, The Author, 1882.

Dwight, Timothy. *Memories of Yale Life and Men, 1845–1899.* New York, Dodd, Mead, 1903.

Edmands, John. *Subjects for Debate, with References to Authorities.* New Haven, 1847.

Foster, William Eaton. "Five Men of '76," American Library Association, *Bulletin,* XX (1926), 312–23.

Gookin, Frederick W. *The Chicago Literary Club; a History of Its First Fifty Years.* Chicago, The Club, 1926.

Green, Samuel Swett. *The Public Library Movement in the United States, 1853–1893.* Boston, Boston Book Co., 1913.

Jewett, Charles Coffin. *Notices of Public Libraries in the United States of America.* Washington, D.C., Smithsonian Institution, 1851.

—— *On the Construction of Catalogues of Libraries, and Their Publication by Means of Separate, Stereotyped Titles; with Rules and Examples.* 2d ed. Washington, D.C., Smithsonian Institution, 1853.

Johnson, Edward. *Wonder-Working Providence of Sion's Saviour in New England,* ed. William Frederick Poole. Andover, Mass., Warren F. Draper, 1867.

Kessler, Sidney H. "William Frederick Poole, Librarian-Historian," *Wilson Library Bulletin,* XXVIII (May, 1954), 788–90.

Mott, Frank Luther. *A History of American Magazines, 1741–1850.* New York, Appleton, 1930.

Newberry Library. Board of Trustees. *Memorial Sketch of Dr. William Frederick Poole.* Chicago, The Library, 1895.

Poole, William Frederick. *An Alphabetical Index to Subjects Treated in the Reviews and Other Periodicals to Which No Indexes Have Been Published.* New York, Putnam, 1848.

—— "Battle of the Dictionaries," *Mercantile Library Reporter,* I (1854–55), 69–72; also published as his *Dictionaries in the Boston*

Mercantile Library and the Boston Athenaeum. Boston, Privately Printed, 1856.

—— "The Early Northwest," American Historical Association, *Papers*, III (1889), 275–300.

—— *An Index to Periodical Literature.* 2d ed. New York, Charles B. Norton, 1853.

—— *An Index to Periodical Literature.* 3d ed. Boston, James R. Osgood, 1882.

—— "The Organization and Management of Public Libraries," in U.S. Bureau of Education, *Public Libraries in the United States, Part I.* Washington, D.C., Government Printing Office, 1876. Pp. 477–98.

—— *The Orthographical Hobgoblin.* Springfield, Mass., Privately Printed, 1859.

—— *Remarks on Library Construction to Which is Appended an Examination of Mr. J. L. Smithmeyer's Pamphlet Entitled "Suggestions on Library Architecture, American and Foreign,"* Chicago, Jansen, McClurg, 1884.

—— "Roosevelt's The Winning of the West," *Atlantic Monthly*, LXIV (November, 1889), 693–700.

—— *The University Library and the University Curriculum.* Chicago, Fleming H. Revell, 1894.

—— *Websterian Orthography; a Reply to Dr. Noah Webster's Calumniators.* Boston, Privately Printed, 1857.

—— "The West from the Treaty of Peace with France, 1763, to the Treaty of Peace with England, 1783," in Justin Winsor, ed. *Narrative and Critical History of America*, Vol. VI. Boston, Houghton, Mifflin, 1887. Pp. 685–743.

—— "Witchcraft in Boston," in Justin Winsor, ed. *Memorial History of Boston*, Vol. II. Boston, James R. Osgood, 1882. Pp. 131–72.

Quincy, Josiah. *The History of the Boston Athenaeum, with Biographical Notices of Its Deceased Founders.* Cambridge, Metcalf, 1851.

Regan, Mary Jane. *Echoes from the Past; Reminiscences of the Boston Athenaeum.* Boston, The Athenaeum, 1927.

Rider, Fremont B. *Melvil Dewey.* Chicago, American Library Association, 1944.

Roden, Carl B. "The Boston Years of Dr. W. F. Poole," in William Warner Bishop and Andrew Keogh, eds. *Essays Offered to Herbert Putnam.* New Haven, Yale University Press, 1929. Pp. 388–94.

—— "Historical Introduction," in Chicago Public Library. *The Chicago Public Library, 1873–1923.* Chicago, The Library, 1923.

Shera, Jesse H. *Foundations of the Public Library.* Chicago, University of Chicago Press, 1949.

Spencer, Gwladys. *The Chicago Public Library; Origins and Background.* Chicago, University of Chicago Press, 1943.

196   *Selected Bibliography*

Thompson, C. Seymour. *Evolution of the American Public Library, 1653–1876.* Washington, D.C., Scarecrow Press, 1952.

U.S. Bureau of Education. *Public Libraries in the United States, Part I.* Washington, D.C., Government Printing Office, 1876.

Utley, George B. *The Librarians' Conference of 1853; a Chapter in American Library History.* Chicago, American Library Association, 1951.

—— "Theodore Roosevelt's *The Winning of the West:* Some Unpublished Letters," *Mississippi Valley Historical Review,* XXX (March, 1944), 495–506.

Wetherold, Houghton. "The Architectural History of the Newberry Library," *Newberry Library Bulletin,* VI (November, 1962), 3–23.

Whitehill, Walter Muir. *Boston Public Library; a Centennial History.* Cambridge, Harvard University Press, 1956.

Yale College. Class of 1849. *Records of the Graduated Members, 1849–1894.* New Haven, The Class, 1895.

Iudex